Mexican Americans

& the U.S. Economy

THE MEXICAN AMERICAN EXPERIENCE

Adela de la Torre,

EDITOR

Other books in the series:

Mexican Americans and Health: ¡Sana! ¡Sana!
  Adela de la Torre & Antonio L. Estrada

Chicano Popular Culture: Que Hable el Pueblo
  Charles M. Tatum

Mexican Americans & the U.S. Economy

Quest for Buenos Días

Arturo González

The University of Arizona Press Tucson

The University of Arizona Press
© 2002 The Arizona Board of Regents

☉ This book is printed on acid-free, archival-quality paper.
Manufactured in the United States of America
First Printing

07   06   05   04   03   02   6   5   4   3   2   1

Library of Congress Cataloging-in-Publication Data
González, Arturo.
    Mexican Americans and the U.S. economy : quest for buenos días / Arturo
González.
        p. cm. — (The Mexican American experience)
    Includes bibliographical references and index.
    ISBN 0-8165-1977-3 (pbk. : acid-free paper)
    1. Mexican Americans—Economic conditions—20th century. 2. Mexican
Americans—Social conditions—20th century. 3. United States—Economic
conditions—1981– 4. United States—Social conditions—1980–
I. Title. II. Series.
    E184.M5 G635 2001
    330.973′.00896872—dc21
    2001002657

British Library Cataloguing-in-Publication Data
A catalogue record for this book is available from the British Library.

For my parents, Daniel and Rosa, and above all, Estella, who was there from the start.

■ CONTENTS

◼ FIGURES

▪ TABLES

Acknowledgments

I would like to thank Adela de la Torre, editor of the Mexican American Experience series, and Patti Hartmann, of the University of Arizona Press, both of whom pointed out ways to improve this work. Patricia Rodriguez assisted with research. In addition, I would like to thank Ngina Chitegi, Jessica Gordon Nembhard, Rhonda Williams, and participants at the "2001 Wealth Inequality in the U.S.A." session at the American Economic Association/Allied Social Science Associations conference, and the "Wealth Accumulation—Global Impacts and Local Prospects: How Race and Ethnicity Matters" conference at the University of Maryland, where I presented chapter 5. *Mil gracias* are also extended to Barbara Robles, of the Lyndon B. Johnson School of Public Affairs at the University of Texas, for discussing and pointing out the many implications of the findings presented in this volume. Lastly, thanks to two anonymous reviewers who provided excellent suggestions.

Mexican Americans

& the U.S. Economy

Overview

MEXICAN AMERICAN PARTICIPATION
IN THE U.S. ECONOMY

The Mexican-origin population in the United States is large and diverse. One reason for this diversity is the sheer size and distribution of the population across the United States. As of March 2000, there are more than 21.7 million Mexican Americans living in the United States, and contrary to popular perceptions, they are not living only in the Southwest. Although figure 1 does indeed show that more than three-quarters of all Mexican Americans live in the southwestern states of California, Texas, and Arizona, there are also large numbers of Mexican Americans living in Illinois, New York, and Michigan, and fairly large numbers in states such as North Carolina and Massachusetts. Using **Mexican American** to refer to all persons of Mexican origin seems to contradict the very cultural, historical, and economic diversity of this population. Therefore, some scholars have made a distinction between Mexicans and Mexican Americans, using the former term to describe U.S.–resident people of Mexican origin who remain closely tied culturally to Mexico and the latter term to describe individuals who have **acculturated** to U.S. society. Yet I do not believe that this distinction necessarily captures the diversity extant among Mexican Americans. Therefore, for the sake of exposition, and without any implied political or cultural ideology, I will use the term **Mexican Americans** to refer to all persons living in the United States who identify themselves as having a Mexican background.

Although Mexican Americans have resided in the United States since before the founding of the United States (in this sense they were Americans before there was such a country), the legacy of racism and continued injustices generally have relegated them to the lower strata of the socioeconomic ladder in U.S. society. Because of their historically marginal and uncertain position in the Southwest, Mexican Americans have only recently emerged as a politically and socially influential ethnic group on a national level. In

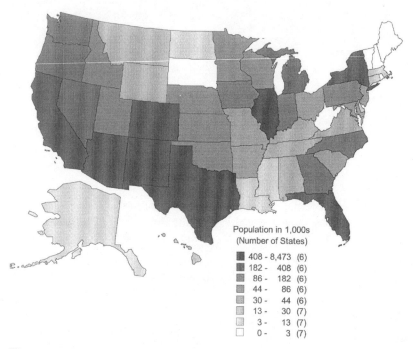

Population in 1,000s
(Number of States)

■	408 - 8,473 (6)
■	182 - 408 (6)
■	86 - 182 (6)
■	44 - 86 (6)
▨	30 - 44 (6)
▨	13 - 30 (7)
▢	3 - 13 (7)
▢	0 - 3 (7)

■ Figure 1. Mexican American population by state of residence (including Washington, D.C.), March 1999. Excludes persons living in group quarters. The numbers in parentheses in the key indicate the number of states in each population category. (Source: Author's weighted tabulations from the March 1999 Current Population Survey)

particular, it has been only in the last half of the twentieth century that Mexican Americans have begun to assert themselves in the U.S. economy.

Historically and presently, the experience of Mexican Americans in the U.S. economy is contradictory. On the positive side, their labor has long been valued and sought by American employers. Indeed, over the twentieth century, Mexican American labor contributed significantly to the economic development of the Southwest, the Midwest, and most recently the South. In addition, Mexican Americans participate in the production of goods and services and pay property, income, and other taxes. As consumers, Mexican Americans are a sizable group. In 1995, their purchasing power totaled more than $117 billion, or about 4 percent of all consumer spending in that year (Paulin 1998, tables 3, 6).

Despite these and other contributions made by Mexican Americans, however, stereotypes persist that Mexican Americans are lazy, unmotivated, and disposable laborers, and that the Mexican American family is foreign and inferior in culture, a drain on public programs and social welfare. In short, these stereotypes portray Mexican Americans as less than fully American. Because so much negative attention is given to particular challenges, such as illegal immigration, high-school dropout rates, poverty, and welfare, it is perhaps not surprising that some have argued Mexican Americans are a permanent **underclass** incapable of joining the ranks of the middle and upper classes.

This ambivalent attitude about Mexican Americans is not a recent phenomenon and most likely is rooted in history. It is well exemplified by the events surrounding the 150th anniversary of the founding of Los Angeles in 1931: Arguing that Mexicans were taking jobs away from Americans during the Great Depression, authorities in Los Angeles deported not only many Mexican immigrants but also U.S.–born Mexican Americans and legal residents, who had long filled the city's labor needs. At the same time, to celebrate the Spanish colonial heritage of Los Angeles, the city's telephone operators greeted callers with "*¡Buenos días!*" Thus, it was completely acceptable to celebrate the legacy of the Spanish and Mexican founders of Los Angeles, but living with them was another matter—authorities had no hesitation about deporting either legal Mexican immigrants or U.S.–born Mexican Americans (Monroy 1999).

The subtitle of this book hints at this ambivalence—how mainstream America celebrates Mexican culture and heritage but at the same time is ambivalent about working and living with Mexican Americans. *Buenos Días* suggests that Mexican Americans are in search not only of "better days" in a literal sense, but also of respect as essential members of American society. Despite the low wages, inadequate education, and many other hardships that Mexican Americans endure, they seek equal opportunities to better themselves. At the same time, they seek the type of warm acceptance and appreciation that Los Angeles telephone operators were so willing to give non-Mexican callers in 1931.

■ Economic Analysis of the Mexican American Population

This book uses economic tools to analyze the position of Mexican Americans in the economy as of March 1999 to argue that Mexican Americans are in the process of attaining economic parity with non-Hispanics. I argue that Mexican Americans do not fare as well economically as non-Hispanic whites for two primary reasons: immigrant status and lower levels of education. In my economic analysis I focus on four topics: (1) immigration, in chapters 2 and 3; (2) educational attainment, in chapter 4; (3) wealth, income, and poverty, in chapter 5; and (4) the labor market, in chapter 6.

The majority of the conclusions are based on data from the U.S. Census Bureau Current Population Survey (CPS) of March 1999, which gathers economic and population information from a representative sample of the population. Although these data provide only a snapshot of the United States at this point in time, the advantages of using them are numerous. In particular, a large, nationally representative sample of Mexican-descent people are included in the survey. This makes it possible to draw conclusions about the nation's Mexican Americans, a feat not always possible in many studies on Mexican Americans. Furthermore, respondents are asked to list the place of birth of their parents, which makes it possible to gauge the economic mobility of Mexican Americans across generations. The CPS is also useful because it covers a wide variety of issues.

I explore the theme that Mexican Americans are striving for buenos días by examining the **socioeconomic status** of first-generation immigrants versus second- and third-generation Mexican Americans. The socioeconomic standing of each generation is compared both in real terms (for example, average work income) and in relative terms (for example, comparing wages of Mexican Americans with those of non-Hispanic whites). By examining three generations it is possible to measure the real gains made by Mexican Americans and to determine whether the socioeconomic situation of Mexican Americans relative to non-Hispanic whites decreases or widens over time.

As I will show in chapters 2 and 3, Mexican immigrants are significantly different from average Americans and from other immigrant groups in many socioeconomic respects; for example, many have less education. These differences place Mexican immigrants and their children at a disadvantage in the U.S. economy, and one would expect Mexican immigrants initially to struggle relative to non-immigrants. The question is, does their economic lot improve with time in the United States, and do the second and third (and higher) generations do better? In fact, in many ways the third generation does better than the second, and the second better than the first, so that each generation cuts into the gap between Mexican Americans and the average American of the same generation.

Demographic Profile of the Mexican American Population

Table 1 provides a general demographic profile of Mexican Americans compared to non–Mexican Americans, revealing that Mexican Americans are worse off in each characteristic listed. These statistics are my motivation to conduct the present economic analysis. In the remainder of this chapter, I will discuss the socioeconomic profile shown in table 1.

In table 1 data are provided for three generations, plus an "Undetermined" category for those whose generation could not be determined, such as individuals born in outlying regions of the United States or Puerto Rico. The first generation comprises foreign-born persons (except individuals born abroad of U.S.–born parents), the second generation comprises U.S.–born persons with at least one foreign-born parent, and the third generation comprises U.S.–born persons with two U.S.–born parents (including those born abroad of U.S.–born parents).

As of March 1999, the Mexican American population was 20.6 million, accounting for more than 8.2 percent of the total U.S. population (and more than 60 percent of all Latinos in the United States). More than 7.2 million of these 20.6 million are first-generation Mexican Americans, and another 6.5 million are the children of at least one immigrant parent. In other words, 13.7 million Mexican Americans, or about 66.5 percent, have an immigrant background, compared to only 16 percent of the largely **assimilated** non-Mexican U.S. population.

Another distinctive characteristic of Mexican Americans is their gender distribution. In all, females comprise 49 percent of all Mexican Americans, whereas this percentage is 51 percent for the rest of the U.S. population. The greatest difference between the two groups occurs in the first generation: 45 percent of Mexican immigrants are females, in contrast to 53 percent of non-Mexican immigrants. Only among third- and undetermined-generation Mexican Americans is the gender distribution similar to that of the non-Mexican-origin population.

Mexican Americans are also younger on average than other Americans. The average age is 26.6 for Mexican American women and 25.9 for men; for non–Mexican Americans, the average ages are 37.0 and 34.8, respectively. Thus, on average, Mexican Americans are nine to ten years younger than the rest of the U.S. population. These differences are particularly

Table 1 Socioeconomic Comparisons of Mexican American and Non–Mexican American Populations, March 1999

		GENERATION			
	Total	First	Second	Third	Undetermined
POPULATION					
Mexican American					
Total	20,635,919	7,240,241	6,495,800	6,539,295	360,583
Percent female	48.7%	45.0%	50.4%	51.0%	51.8%
Non–Mexican American					
Total	250,909,254	19,218,044	20,667,396	207,240,299	3,783,515
Percent female	51.3%	52.5%	51.4%	51.2%	52.2%
AVERAGE AGE					
Mexican American					
Male	25.9	33.4	18.1	24.3	28.4
Female	26.6	35.5	18.4	25.6	30.9
Non–Mexican American					
Male	34.8	40.9	36.2	34.1	32.9
Female	37.0	43.1	39.4	36.3	33.2
AVERAGE HIGHEST GRADE COMPLETED (IF 25 YEARS OR OLDER)					
Mexican American					
Male	10.1	8.8	11.6	12.0	10.7
Female	10.1	8.5	11.4	11.8	9.8
Non–Mexican American					
Male	13.2	13.1	13.5	13.2	12.2
Female	13.0	12.6	12.9	13.0	12.1
LABOR FORCE STATUS (15 YEARS AND OLDER, NOT IN ARMED FORCES)					
Mexican American					
Employed	62.7%	61.2%	46.3%	64.5%	57.8%
Unemployed	4.7%	4.5%	5.2%	4.8%	3.0%
Non–Mexican American					
Employed	61.9%	62.8%	55.0%	64.5%	67.2%
Unemployed	2.9%	3.2%	2.2%	2.9%	4.7%
AVERAGE FAMILY SIZE					
Mexican American	3.9	4.2	3.4	3.6	4.1
Non–Mexican American	3.1	3.4	2.7	3.0	3.3
AVERAGE 1998 HOUSEHOLD INCOME, BY HOUSEHOLDER TYPE					
Mexican American					
Husband-Wife	$43,257	$36,085	$49,497	$53,314	$46,557
Male	$39,942	$42,522	$37,219	$35,970	$38,160
Female	$23,636	$19,309	$27,218	$25,862	$24,355
Non–Mexican American					
Husband-Wife	$69,439	$69,202	$73,200	$69,347	$55,875
Male	$49,172	$49,192	$59,329	$48,663	$36,610
Female	$32,073	$32,179	$41,931	$31,492	$29,960

Source: Author's weighted tabulations from the March 1999 Current Population Survey.
Notes: Only primary families are counted, where appropriate. Excludes persons living in group quarters.

stark in the second generation, where Mexican Americans average eighteen years of age, compared to nearly thirty-eight years for non–Mexican Americans.

The youthfulness of the population has numerous policy implications. In terms of health, Mexican Americans will tend to be healthier and to have different needs from the health-care system than the non-Mexican-origin population. With regard to the labor market, younger individuals require more job training, are more likely to switch jobs, and generally earn less. Finally, young taxpayers in the labor force help support older and retired individuals.

Overall Mexican Americans are less educated than non–Mexican Americans, averaging ten years of schooling, but this is greatly influenced by generational status. For example, at the low extreme, first-generation Mexican Americans have an average educational level of less than nine years, whereas the second generation averages about 11.5 years, and the third generation, a high-school diploma (twelve years). Yet even third-generation Mexican Americans lag behind the average of thirteen years for the rest of the population. These findings raise several questions for educators: What are the factors behind the lower education of Mexican Americans? What programs need to be improved or expanded to increase the educational attainment of Mexican Americans? What is the cost of these programs? Are Mexican Americans **assimilating** (reaching parity) in education?

Generally, individuals with low levels of education have adverse labor market characteristics. However, table 1 reveals that the labor force status of Mexican Americans does not always conform to this prediction: Mexican Americans have higher levels of **labor force participation** (working or seeking work) than the rest of the population—67.4 percent compared to 64.8 percent. Mexican Americans are dedicated to working or at least seeking work.

Unfortunately, another reason for the high labor force participation of Mexican Americans is their higher **unemployment rate**. That is, since labor force participation encompasses people who are either working or actively seeking work, the large number of Mexican Americans seeking work partially accounts for their higher participation. Mexican Americans are about 1.6 times more likely than non–Mexican Americans to be unemployed (4.7 percent compared to 2.9 percent). The implication is that Mexican Americans are willing to work, if given the opportunity, but that they have more difficulty finding and keeping a job than non–Mexican Americans do. These unemployment figures challenge policymakers to provide training or resources that aid Mexican Americans in their job search.

Family size is another distinguishing characteristic of Mexican Americans. Whereas the average Mexican American family averages nearly four persons, the non-Mexican-origin family averages three persons. Note that the difference is greatest in the first generation and lowest in the third generation. Moreover, the Mexican American household (whether it be a single-parent or two-parent household) has a lower income than the corresponding non–Mexican American household, with the differences in incomes ranging from $8,400 for female-headed households to $26,200 for married households. Again, the differences in income level between Mexican Americans and non–Mexican Americans tend to be less for the third generation and for those of undetermined generation.

The combination of lower income and larger family size for the Mexican American household results in higher **poverty status.** Because fewer dollars are spread over more individuals in Mexican American households, they have a lower per-capita (per-person) income. The implications of poverty are significant; poverty is at the root of many social inequities. For example, children growing up in poor households are more likely, on average, to live in socially underprivileged areas. Given these statistics, some scholars have portrayed Mexican Americans as trapped in a cycle of poverty that prevents them from moving into the **middle class** (the underclass model). A goal of this book is to point out the progress, or lack thereof, that Mexican Americans make from one generation to the next. I argue throughout that Mexican Americans are not an underclass; rather they are making progress across generations toward achieving the American dream.

 Outline for *Mexican Americans and the U.S. Economy*

The following chapters will examine the issues raised in the preceding section, although those with undetermined generational status are omitted from the rest of the analysis. Given the large number of first- and second-generation Mexican Americans, chapter 2 provides an economic analysis and brief historical background of Mexican immigration. Building upon this foundation, chapter 3 examines contemporary immigration issues, including the impact of immigration on the U.S. economy. Chapter 4 details the educational status of Mexican Americans, and provides some explanations for the different educational outcomes of Mexican Americans and non–Mexican Americans. Chapter 5 examines the income of Mexican Americans, as well as issues surrounding income, including poverty and the acquisition of **wealth.** Chapter 6 examines the labor market situation of Mexican Americans. Lastly, chapter 7 concludes with a summary of what has been learned.

In addition, each chapter demonstrates how Mexican Americans have long been a part of American economic systems and that long-held negative stereotypes are mostly baseless. The statistics reveal a people who are improving themselves and reducing the gap between themselves and non-Hispanic whites. Such information will complement the breadth of knowledge acquired in other courses and texts on Mexican Americans.

Each chapter begins with a vignette or quotation chosen to illustrate the topic of the chapter. Each chapter also includes a topic highlight that illuminates a particular issue, generally in the form of a case study or example. These highlights help show how economics can be used to gain further insight into the experiences of Mexican Americans. Key terms, which appear in the glossary, are in boldface on first use in each chapter.

■ Discussion Questions

1. What is the thesis of the book? Based on what you know now, would you agree or disagree with it?

2. What is the source for most of the data used in this book, and what aspects of these data are used? When were these data collected? What might be the limitations of using these data?

3. Name at least three demographic differences between Mexican Americans and non–Mexican Americans.

4. What policy implications arise from these demographic differences? Think of implications in addition to those described in the text.

◼ Suggested Readings

Meier, Matt S., and Feliciano Ribera. 1993. *Mexican Americans/American Mexicans.* New York: Hill and Wang.

Sánchez, George J. 1993. *Becoming Mexican American.* New York: Oxford University Press.

Vélez-Ibáñez, Carlos G. 1996. *Border Visions: Mexican Culture of the Southwest United States.* Tucson: University of Arizona Press.

2

Al Norte

ECONOMIC PRINCIPLES OF
MEXICAN IMMIGRATION

Because of my childhood, I always wanted to go to the United States. I thought about it all the time. It was my dream to go north to work and return home with clothes for my mother and all my brothers and sisters. (Jorge Urroz, quoted in Rothenberg 1998, 122)

We all saw how the **braceros** came back with the good clothes for their families and nice shoes. They said that they suffered a lot in the United States, but I saw how much better they lived. I wanted the same. I thought to myself, "God willing, I'm going to the United States too." (Norberto Herrera, quoted in Rothenberg 1998, 37)

Centuries before the Southwest became part of the United States in 1848, Mexican and Spanish settlers migrated from the interior of Mexico to the northern provinces of New Spain, including areas that are now in the states of California, Texas, and New Mexico. From the U.S.–Mexico War in 1848 until about 1910, Mexican immigration to the United States went relatively unnoticed. For many, the border established by the **Treaty of Guadalupe Hidalgo** in 1848 and the **Gadsden Purchase** in 1853 was more an imaginary than a real boundary. During the nineteenth century, it was not uncommon for Mexicans and Mexican Americans to cross from one country to the other without worrying about border checkpoints (Meier and Ribera 1993; Sánchez 1993).

Yet, more Mexicans have immigrated to the United States since 1980 than in the previous 150 years. As figure 2 shows there were more than 7.5 million Mexican immigrants in 1999, of which more than 5.2 million arrived between 1980 and 1999. This means that 68.9 percent of current Mexican immigrants arrived in this twenty-year period. Even after accounting for mortality and return migration of pre-1980 immigrants, this percentage is extremely large and is higher than that for non-Mexican

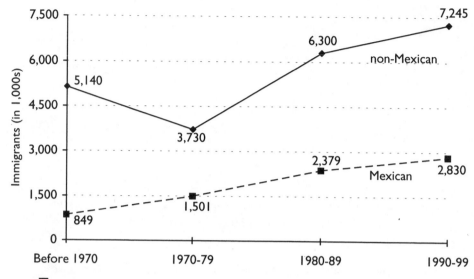

Figure 2. Year of entry for immigrants to the United States. (Source: Author's weighted tabulations from the March 1999 Current Population Survey)

immigrants, 60.4 percent of whom entered in the 1980–1999 period. Despite the fact that the number of Mexican immigrants entering the country is as large as at any time in history, much of the current migration flow is an outcome of past immigration patterns, including the establishment of settlement, employment, and social networks, primarily in the Southwest but also in other parts of the country such as the Midwest (Vargas 1993).

In 1960, immigrants constituted about 15 percent of the Mexican American population (compared to 35 percent in 1999), and hence the influence of Mexican culture relative to American culture was less than it is now. Currently, Mexican immigrants reinvigorate and reinforce the Mexican culture in Mexican American neighborhoods of cities such as Chicago, Los Angeles, and San Antonio. As such, Mexican immigrants help retard the process of **assimilation** to U.S. culture, and encourage the development of a bicultural (Mexican and American) and bilingual (English and Spanish) population. The relationship between Mexican Americans and other Americans is clouded by this facet of immigration. Mexican Americans may be considered as less than true Americans, and their Mexican cultural maintenance is often used as an excuse to discriminate against or to disassociate from them.

For these reasons, as well as to gain a better understanding of who Mexican Americans are today and who they will be tomorrow, an economic analysis of Mexican immigration is useful. This chapter first presents an economic model of the migration decision for Mexican immigrants. It then summarizes the history of Mexican immigration to the United States, which can be broken down into four periods or waves: (1) pre-1910, (2) 1910 to 1929, (3) 1942 to 1964, and (4) post-1964.

■ Why Do People Immigrate?

In 1995, after adjusting for differences in the purchasing power of the dollar in the United States and Mexico (because a dollar buys more in Mexico than in the United States), the per-capita **gross national product** (GNP) of the United States was $27,000, versus $6,400 in Mexico (World Bank 1997). Combined with the lengthy shared U.S.–Mexico border and the established **international migration networks,** this fourfold difference in adjusted GNP is a **pull factor** that motivates Mexicans to migrate. Other pull factors that play a role in the migration decision include, but are not limited to, employment opportunities in the United States, social networks (friends from one's hometown), and social services (unemployment insurance, health services). For people like Jorge Urroz and Norberto Herrera, the decision to emigrate from their small *ranchos* in Mexico was based partly on the stories and experiences of previous immigrants as well as the existence of social networks that facilitate travel and settlement in the United States.

In addition, numerous aspects of life in Mexico, such as poverty, economic downturns, and political strife, are **push factors** that encourage many Mexicans to migrate north to the United States—**el norte**—in search of a better life.

Despite the obvious economic gains to be made from immigrating, the decision to immigrate is not an easy one. Not only does it mean leaving behind family members, friends, and other loved ones, but the immigrant must find a way to finance the trip, and then adjust to a new language, culture, land, and labor market after immigrating. For **undocumented immigrants**, the decision to immigrate is particularly difficult because the journey involves finding a way to cross the border, risking robbery, assault, rape, or even death, and facing exploitation by Mexican and American border officials, and unscrupulous employers in the United States (Annerino 1999). Despite the hardships and dangers, hundreds of thousands make the journey north every year, both legally and illegally.

Just as it is impossible to identify all the push and pull factors, it is equally difficult to ascertain the exact influence of these factors on the decision to immigrate. Although individuals consider many external factors in their migration decisions, only a certain segment of the Mexican population chooses to immigrate, whereas others choose to remain in Mexico. In other words, even though the same push-pull factors act upon the whole Mexican population, only a specific segment of the population immigrates. Why do some stay and others leave?

With the exception of political refugees in the early twentieth century, the majority of Mexican immigrants have emigrated for better economic opportunities, for which wages are the best proxy (stand-in measure for something that cannot be measured directly). However, if wages are indeed the primary reason behind immigration, why do the majority of Mexican workers not emigrate to the United States? A more sophisticated and realistic analysis considers the *relative* wages of potential immigrants; that is, it factors in the monetary and non-monetary costs of immigration to determine whether, for a particular individual, potential wages in the United States are still greater relative to the wages earned in Mexico. Thus, each Mexican must consider his or her wages versus the costs of leaving. Those whose *relative net wages* are greater in the United States will immigrate. Furthermore, recent evidence suggests that, at least for undocumented immigrants, the decision to migrate is more sensitive to a decline in Mexican wages than to changes in American wages (Hanson and Spilimbergo 1999).

It turns out that Mexicans with low education levels are better off coming to the United States, whereas Mexicans with higher levels of education are better off staying in Mexico. The chapter appendix presents a formal model showing this result. Because the push-pull factors affect Mexicans differently, the average Mexican immigrant tends to be poorly educated rather than highly educated. Another important conclusion of the model is that toughening immigration laws actually acts to *lower* the average education level of the immigrant flow. Tougher laws increase the risks and costs of migrating, meaning that the benefits of immigration outweigh the costs only for people with relatively low levels of education.

In light of these findings, it is not surprising that the **Immigration Reform and Control Act** (IRCA)—which imposed sanctions on U.S. employers who hired undocumented workers—failed to stop illegal immigration. Immigrants come to the United States primarily because there are relatively fewer economic opportunities in Mexico, rather than because the economic opportunities in the United States are better. Given the harsh reality of Mexico's economic situation, certain Mexicans have no choice but to seek better opportunities in el norte.

■ Immigration before 1910

The first foreigners to cross the U.S.–Mexico border legally and illegally in large numbers were Americans wanting to begin new lives in Texas in 1821. In that year Stephen Austin, leading a group of American settlers, founded the city of Austin. Their motivation was land grants provided by the Mexican government, which was trying to encourage settlement of its sparsely populated northern provinces of California, New Mexico, and Texas. In the 1820s, for example, the largest province, New Mexico, had an estimated population of about five thousand people (Meier and Ribera 1993). After successive Spanish and Mexican governments had failed to persuade their citizens to migrate north, Mexico sought American settlers to offset threats posed by French, English, and other foreign governments' interest in the northern territories. However, in order to qualify for land grants, Americans had to agree to various conditions, including Mexican citizenship and conversion to Catholicism, to insure their loyalty to Mexico. Despite numerous attempts to control legal American immigration, many Americans settled illegally in Texas due to the economic opportunities found there.

Prior to the discovery of gold in California in 1849, Mexicans generally were not attracted to the present-day Southwest. Once Mexicans from the mining states of Sonora and Zacatecas began arriving in large numbers in the last half of the nineteenth century, California, a brand-new U.S. territory, passed laws prohibiting Mexicans, including those who had lived there since Spanish colonial times, from staking claims to mines (Meier and Ribera 1993). Despite the open hostility toward Mexicans, by the late nineteenth century there were as many Mexicans as *californios* (people of Mexican/Spanish descent born in California). The majority of this migration took place between towns along the U.S.–Mexico border.

■ Revolution and Economic Growth: 1910–1929

Despite the lack of an extensive recorded history of Mexican migration during the late nineteenth century, political and economic changes were taking place on both sides of the border that would create the incentives and opportunities for immigration from Mexico at the turn of the century. The economic policies implemented during the dictatorship of **Porfirio Díaz** (1876–1911) had lasting impacts on the Mexican people. El Porfiriato—the name given to the policies and tenure of Díaz—resulted in unprecedented economic changes in Mexico aimed at modernizing the country. The economic growth was accomplished partly by transferring small plots of lands from peasants to large landowners, increasing foreign investment, and developing an extensive railroad system to transport products and foods to distant markets within Mexico and the United States (Monroy 1999; Sánchez 1993).

The negative consequences of these modernization policies hurt in particular Mexico's poor. The land reforms that consolidated small ranchos into large *haciendas,* and the unequal distribution of income and profits, transformed many peasant farmers into indebted peons, forcing them to work for wealthy farmers as sharecroppers or as wage earners. By the time of the Mexican Revolution in 1910, it was not uncommon for rural peasants to earn from ten to twenty-five cents a day (J. González 1985; Monroy 1999; Sánchez 1993). As a consequence of these economic policies that enriched the wealthy but not the poor, many peasants lived a meager existence. As a result of price increases for food staples such as corn, along with a doubling in the population, malnutrition was not uncommon among Mexico's poor. Prior to El Porfiriato they at least had been able to live off their own land (Monroy 1999).

Díaz's goal was to modernize the domestic economy through growth in the export sector. One of the accomplishments of his dictatorship was the construction of a modern and extensive railroad system that connected more than fifteen thousand miles of track (Sánchez 1993). Most of this construction occurred in the mining states of Mexico and other north-central states, such as Michoacán, Zacatecas, Durango, and Jalisco (Hamann 1999). The consensus is that Mexico achieved some level of industrialization it would not otherwise have achieved. This accomplishment is often cited to point out the good intentions and accomplishments of Díaz. Recent evidence, however, suggests that the growth in exports did not have lasting effects on key sectors of the economy (Catão 1998). Thus, it may be that the wealthy accrued only short-term benefits, while the poor did not benefit in either the short or long run.

The cumulative effect of land reforms, unequal economic growth, and political oppression was an organized revolt in 1910. When Francisco Madero initiated a widespread revolt against Díaz in 1910, many peasants were caught in the middle. Due to widespread fighting in many rural areas of Mexico, rural lands could not be farmed. Continual fighting between government and rebel armies also resulted in economic distress, high inflation, and general disruption in everyday economic activity, which worsened an already marginal existence for many Mexicans (Monroy 1999; Sánchez 1993). Facing physical danger as well as an inability to feed their families, many Mexicans near railroad lines chose to leave their homes and travel north.

The Mexican Revolution thus precipitated the first large wave of Mexican immigration. Official figures underestimate the number of Mexicans who entered the United States, as only legal immigrants were counted. Nevertheless, even official figures point to a large exodus during the revolutionary period: whereas only 53,000 Mexicans legally entered the United States from 1881 to 1910, more than 219,000 entered from 1911 to 1920. Continued political instability, including the Cristero War of the late 1920s, led an additional 459,000 to enter the United States from 1921 to 1930 (Meier and Ribera 1993).

Just as conditions in Mexico were driving many to emigrate, economic conditions in the United States encouraged many Mexicans to remain in the United States, and encouraged others to follow. Before Mexicans became the primary ethnic workforce in the Southwest, Chinese and Japanese immigrants had constituted the mainstay in agriculture, railroad, and other manual-labor-intensive jobs. Ethnic prejudice and racism against Asian immigrants resulted in restrictive immigration legislation and voluntary restrictions that essentially ended immigration from Asia in the late nineteenth century (Meier and Ribera 1993).

Yet the expansion of railroads, mining, and agriculture in the Southwest at the turn of the century increased the demand for labor. For example, during the 1920s, irrigation of California's Central Valley began the transformation of an arid region into the world's leading agricultural region (Meier and Ribera 1993; Sánchez 1993). The large number of new Mexican immigrants helped fill the growing demand for workers. Without such an abundant and cheap workforce, it is questionable whether the region would have developed as quickly or as extensively.

By 1900, southern Europeans had replaced northern Europeans as the predominant immigrant nationalities. As the proportion of these immigrants reached 14 percent in the 1910s (a percentage still unmatched by the present wave of immigration), Americans of northern European ancestry feared that the new immigrants would not assimilate or adopt the American ideals of democracy and the Protestant work ethic. In an attempt to halt this changing ethnic composition of the U.S. population, the United States began to impose limits on legal immigration (Freeman and Bean 1997). The passage of legislation restricting the number of immigrants began in the late 1910s and culminated with the National Origins Quota Act in 1924. This act allocated visas to European and Eastern Hemisphere countries based on the country-of-origin composition of the United States in 1890, a year when northern and western European Americans dominated (DeSipio and de la Garza, 1998).

The racist attitudes against immigrants extended to Mexicans, who had long been seen as inferior by many Americans. Numerous attempts were made to include Mexicans in the series of restrictive immigration acts of the period. However, southwestern employers, who needed a pool of cheap and effective workers, constituted a special-interest group that succeeded in excluding Mexicans from numerical quotas until the 1960s. As a result, Mexicans escaping political and economic hardships in Mexico did not find it difficult to find employment. The majority found employment in the mines of Arizona and New Mexico; the agricultural fields of Texas, California, and the Midwest; or the railroad lines of the Southwest (Meier and Ribera 1993). Today, many immigrant-receiving communities throughout the United States can trace their origins to the 1910s (Monroy 1999; Monto 1994; Sánchez 1993).

■ The Depression and Bracero Eras: 1930–1964

The first large wave of Mexican immigration came to an end when the stock market crashed in October 1929, and the economic conditions that had enabled Mexicans to live and work in the United States disappeared. The decline in native employment led to the deportation of many Mexican immigrants in the early 1930s. Although the majority of those returned to

Mexico were legal and undocumented immigrants, U.S.–born Mexicans were also "encouraged" to leave the United States. American organizations and government agencies used methods ranging from financial assistance with the return trip to Mexico to outright civil rights violations (Monroy 1999). In all, it is estimated that one-quarter to one-half million Mexicans were returned to Mexico during the 1930s (Meier and Ribera 1993).

Once the United States entered World War II, however, the demand for labor skyrocketed and Mexico once again became a source of cheap labor. Increased government spending to fund the war allowed American citizens who were unemployed or working in low-paying occupations to find employment in high-paying manufacturing industries in urban centers. The need to feed Allied soldiers coincided with a reduction in the agricultural and rural workforce in the United States. To resolve the labor shortage, the U.S. and Mexican governments in 1942 implemented a temporary-worker program called the Bracero Accord. Under this accord, Mexican workers were to be recruited in Mexico for seasonal work in the United States, usually under contracts that lasted less than eight months (García y Griego 1996). Although intended as a wartime measure, the Bracero Program did not end until 1964.

The purpose of the program was to provide a steady supply of workers, mostly for agricultural concerns although railroad companies also participated in the program. The Mexican government was initially reluctant, fearing that the loss of workers would hurt Mexico's economy. To the contrary, however, emigration out of Mexico helped reduce the effects of unemployment, low wages, and poverty there. As all braceros worked under seasonal contacts and intended to return to Mexico, the majority saved a large portion of their income and sent remittances (money orders, wire transfers) to their families. This was to the braceros' advantage because the dollar could buy far more in Mexico than in the United States (World Bank 1997), and money received by the braceros' families helped rejuvenate entire Mexican communities. The image of a thrifty or Spartan Mexican immigrant was solidified by braceros.

The Bracero Program not only continued at the end of the war, it was expanded in the postwar era. The reason for this was simple; the program benefited all sides: American companies found a steady supply of workers at reasonable rates, American consumers paid relatively low prices for the products, braceros earned more money to support their families, and the

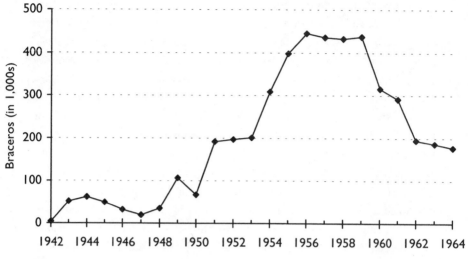

Figure 3. Number of braceros for fiscal years 1942 to 1964. (Source: García y Griego 1996)

Mexican government found a "safety valve" for its high **unemployment** and poverty rates. As a consequence of lobbying efforts in Congress by farming interests, the Bracero Program was renewed annually until 1964. Figure 3 shows the growth of the program over the course of the twenty-three years of its existence. It reached its peak in the late 1950s, when more than 400,000 workers per year came to the United States.

The End of the Bracero Program and Its Legacy

If the Bracero Program was so beneficial, why was it terminated? Although beneficial to many groups, the program was also criticized by certain segments of the American population and by the Mexican government (García y Griego 1996). Many of the criticisms centered around the abysmal working and housing conditions of migrant workers, issues of discrimination and racism, and the complaint by the Mexican government that the U.S. government ignored undocumented Mexican immigrants who undermined the Bracero Program by accepting wages and working conditions below the standard set by the act. Although the bracero legislation stipulated that braceros could not be used as replacement workers, only as supplementary labor when needed, many in the Mexican American labor movement argued that American employers used braceros to restrict employment and wage opportunities for Mexican American labor. One of the leading forces in this protest was the National Farm Workers Association, later the United Farm Workers, led by César Chávez.

Over time, these problems attracted much negative publicity. By the 1960s, significant political pressure to end the program was coming from unions, Mexican American labor activists, and civic and church organizations. Only strong lobbying efforts by farm interests kept the program alive from year to year. Many employers, sensitive to public perceptions regarding the mistreatment of braceros, chose not to lobby vigorously for renewal of the program in the late 1950s and early 1960s. Consequently the number of braceros began to decrease (see figure 3). Finally, in 1963 the U.S. Congress decided to renew the program for only one more year, and the Bracero Program came to an end on December 31, 1964.

The legacy of the Bracero Program on Mexican immigration was long-lasting and established many patterns found in the present-day immigration stream. In particular, it established an immigration stream from Mexico that is both seasonal and cyclical. Immigrants would work for a number of months in the United States, return to Mexico, and then repeat the process again after several months. This is one aspect of Mexican immigration that is different from immigration from other countries. Whereas immigrants from countries in Europe, Asia, or South America are more likely to relocate to the United States permanently, the close proximity of Mexico enables Mexican immigrants to make repeated trips back and forth from Mexico.

The typical pattern of Mexican immigration can be described as occurring in three phases: (1) a sojourner phase, (2) a transitional phase, and (3) a settlement phase (Massey 1986). Immigrants in the sojourner phase enter the United States alone to work. They are target-income earners, hold unstable and seasonal jobs, and send the majority of their income home to Mexico. As a consequence they live a Spartan existence, work long hours, and have little interest in developing ties to the local community.

During the transitional phase, the continued trips north lead the immigrant to begin developing social ties in the United States and make family separation more difficult to accept. With more labor market experience and knowledge of social networks in the United States, the immigrant attains better jobs and wages and begins spending more time in the United States.

In the settlement phase, the immigrant arranges for family members to join him or her in the United States. The family develops closer ties to local communities and to formal institutions, such as schools, banks, and government agencies. Further knowledge of the labor market and increased skills, such as ability to speak English, lead to better job opportunities and higher wages. As a consequence, the majority of the family income is spent in the United States.

Another legacy of the Bracero Program is the continued development of the international migration networks that were established by the waves of immigrants during the Mexican Revolution. As previously noted, early immigrants made their way north using the various railroad lines. It is no coincidence, then, that the majority of pre-1964 immigrants came from the six to eight Mexican states along the railroad lines (García y Griego 1996). The initial wave of immigrants developed knowledge regarding employment, housing, and cultural receptiveness. In addition, they also developed and became more familiar with methods of entering the country, both legally and illegally. When these early immigrants returned to their hometowns, they shared their experiences with others who were weighing the benefits and hardships of undertaking the journey north. Even eighty years after these early immigrants made their initial journeys north, new immigrants from the same town are immigrating mostly as a result of the migration networks established then (Hamann 1999; Monto 1994).

These social networks serve to reduce the monetary and non-monetary costs associated with immigration. New immigrants oftentimes leave their hometown either because someone provided information about available jobs or because they know either a person or community of immigrants that can offer shelter, help in finding a job, and social support. These networks also facilitate the transmission of information regarding border-crossing points and the process of applying for legal residency, as well as help in paying for a **coyote** or **pollero** (a smuggler of undocumented immigrants).

■ The Immigration and Nationality Act of 1965

The end of the Bracero Program coincided with a significant change in immigration policy in the United States. The Immigration and Nationality Act of 1965 replaced the National Origins Quota Act of 1924. Under the previous act, visas had been allocated to countries based on the national composition of the United States in 1890 (DeSipio and de la Garza 1998).

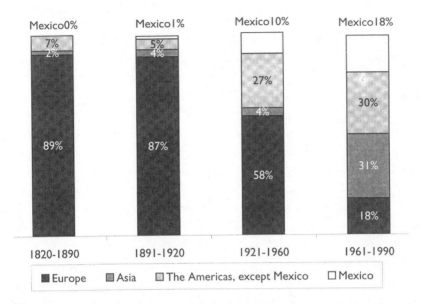

Mexico0%	Mexico1%	Mexico10%	Mexico18%
7%	5%		
2%	4%	27%	30%
		4%	
89%	87%	58%	31%
			18%
1820-1890	1891-1920	1921-1960	1961-1990

■ Europe   ■ Asia   ☐ The Americas, except Mexico   ☐ Mexico

■ Figure 4. Region of origin of immigrants, 1820–1990. (Source: U.S. Immigration and Naturalization Service 1997)

This resulted in the majority of visas going to western and northern European countries. In contrast, the 1965 immigration act established family connections and work skills as the primary qualifying criteria. The act also placed a limit for the first time on the number of visas allocated per country at twenty thousand. An important feature of the act that affected immigration to the United States for the next twenty-five years was that family members of U.S. citizens and legal residents received 80 percent of all visas, and immigrants admitted under this **family-preference provision** were not subject to the visa limitations. Both the per-country and category preference system initially applied only to the Eastern Hemisphere, but both were applied to the Western Hemisphere beginning in 1976.

As a consequence of this change in immigration policy, the composition of immigrants changed substantially after 1965. Figure 4 shows the region of origin for legal immigrants from 1820 to 1990. Clearly, before 1960, the majority of immigrants were from European countries. The percentage of legal immigrants from Mexico remained less than 1 percent until after 1920, when the percentage of European immigrants declined despite the passage of the National Origins Quota Act. Only after the Bracero Program was implemented did Mexico begin to contribute a significant percentage of the total legal immigrant population. After the passage of the immigration act of 1965, the share of Mexicans in the legal immigrant population rose to 18 percent and remains at 20 percent as of 1998 (U.S. Immigration and Naturalization Service [hereafter INS] 1999a, 8). In this period Mexico has accounted for the same percentage of legal immigrants as all European countries combined.

The surge in the number of Mexican immigrants since the 1960s is largely attributable to the family reunification provisions in the immigration laws, continued economic problems in Mexico, and economic opportunities in the United States. The initial settlement of political refugees during the Mexican Revolution and social networks strengthened by the Bracero Program also facilitated immigration. Since family members were exempt from the country-specific quotas, Mexicans with eligible immediate relatives (a parent, child, or sibling) who were legal U.S. residents could immigrate with little difficulty. This resulted in a domino effect (sometimes referred to as *chain migration*), as newly admitted immigrants then sponsored their immediate relatives, and so on.

While legal immigration increased sharply, illegal immigration also rose during this time. During the Bracero Program, the United States dealt with undocumented immigrants by legalizing, deporting, or ignoring them. With the end of the program, however, immigrants interested in seasonal employment rather than permanent residence could no longer apply for work permits. They had to rely on the formal immigrant application process: (1) apply for the visas allocated to Mexico, (2) be sponsored by an immediate relative, or (3) have occupational skills that qualify them for employment-based preferences. (In general, Mexican immigrants are not treated as refugees, and hence that aspect of immigration law is not relevant for them.) Immigrants who could not immediately obtain legal residency used social networks to enter the United States illegally. The topic of undocumented immigration is discussed in more detail in the next chapter.

■ The Immigration Reform and Control Act of 1986

Although undocumented immigration had always been part of the history of Mexican immigration, it was not until the 1970s, and especially the 1980s, that it became a heated political and social topic. Prior to this time, the U.S. government had dealt with undocumented immigrants by granting them legal status several times in the 1950s, by administratively legalizing them as braceros throughout the program's existence, and by ignoring them during the 1960s.

Beginning especially in the mid-1960s, the number of applicants from Mexico exceeded the available visas, and not all Mexicans seeking to immigrate qualified under the family or employment preference classes. By 1980, there were nearly 200,000 Mexicans on waiting lists for the available visas, which translated into almost a ten-year wait (Meier and Ribera 1993). Given the high demand for visas, the existence of social and migration networks and a cyclical migration pattern, and the lack of a formal process to accommodate workers, it is not surprising that the number of undocumented Mexican immigrants rose to between 2.5 and 3.5 million during the 1980s. It is estimated that around 50 percent of all current undocumented immigrants are Mexican (INS 1997).

Following the economic recession of the 1970s and 1980s and the budgetary problems of many local and state governments in the 1980s, undocumented immigrants, along with other ethnic and national groups, became easy scapegoats for social problems. Certain segments of the U.S. population believed and argued that undocumented immigrants took jobs away from U.S. citizens and legal residents, were a drain on social services, were a major source of crime, and threatened the national sovereignty of the country. A series of bills were introduced in the U.S. Congress in an attempt to curb the growing number of undocumented immigrants. The culmination of these actions was the IRCA of 1986.

This piece of legislation contained two major provisions aimed at substantially reducing future undocumented immigration while simultaneously dealing with those already in the country in a humanitarian manner. Believing that undocumented immigration was driven primarily by the attraction of jobs, the authors of IRCA thought that imposing **employer sanctions,** or legal penalties against employers, would eliminate the pull of U.S. jobs. Prior to IRCA, it was not illegal for U.S. employers to hire undocumented workers, although it was illegal for the immigrant to be in the country without a work permit or visa.

Under the 1986 law, employers are required to verify whether potential employees are legally permitted to work in the United States. Those that *knowingly* hire undocumented immigrants are subject to fines or imprisonment. As a consequence, workers now have to prove they have a legal right to work by providing documents such as a driver's license and a Social Security card, a U.S. passport, a "green card," or other approved legal document. Although this provision places the burden on employers to judge the authenticity of U.S. legal documents presented to them, the official Form I-9 for recording the verification states that an employer simply has to inspect the documents and judge them to be "genuine."

The impact of the employer sanctions has been predictable. Rather than making employers the enforcers of U.S. immigration laws, IRCA has created a black market in false documents. For the right price, undocumented immigrants can acquire false Social Security cards, driver's licenses, and other documents that will satisfy an employer. Furthermore, even if employers may know or suspect that they are hiring undocumented workers, they now have official forms to prove that they were given proof of the worker's legal status! As long as employers keep up the illusion that they have no knowledge of the undocumented status of their workers, they are not likely to be fined. Ironically, the U.S. government has provided employers with the legal means by which to disguise their hiring of undocumented workers.

In summary, although the intent of IRCA was to impose an obstacle to undocumented immigration, employer sanctions did not accomplish this. In essence, IRCA simply raised the cost of undocumented immigration by an amount equal to the cost of obtaining false documents plus the costs resulting from increased border enforcement. The cumulative effect of IRCA on the flow of undocumented immigrants has been minimal. In fact, the INS estimates that in 1996 about 2.7 million out of a total of about 5 million undocumented immigrants in the United States were Mexican (INS 1999b).

The other major aspect of IRCA was an **amnesty** provision that legalized the status of undocumented immigrants who had been living in the United States for some time. Included under this provision were long-term residents, defined as those who had lived continuously in the United States since January 1, 1982, and agricultural workers who had worked at least ninety days in 1985–1986 or ninety days since 1983 and had resided in the United States for ninety days. The provisions for agricultural workers created a category of immigrants known as Special Agricultural Worker (SAW) immigrants, to satisfy agricultural interests.

In all, more than 3 million immigrants qualified for amnesty and received legal residence. Of these, about 2.3 million were Mexican, with more than 1 million qualifying under the regular amnesty provisions and another 1.3 million under the SAW provision (DeFreitas 1991). It would not be surprising that newly legalized immigrants then sponsored the immigration of their family members to the United States. Therefore, the overall impact of the IRCA amnesty provisions on Mexican immigration is probably significantly greater than 2.3 million.

Recent Legislation

The Immigration Act of 1990 placed numerical limits on family-sponsored immigration for the first time and capped total immigration at 675,000 per year (INS 1999a). Furthermore, family-sponsored immigrants could constitute only about 71 percent of the total visas. (The actual number of visas issued to family members was 480,000 minus the number of visas issued during the previous year to immediate relatives of immigrants, plus unused employment-based visas with a minimum of 226,000 visas to be given during any given year.) This methodology essentially limited family-based legal immigration in the year following a surge in family-based immigration.

Fueled by continued xenophobia and the desire to find a convenient scapegoat for the nation's problems with legal and illegal immigrants, Congress passed the Illegal Immigration Reform and Immigration Responsibility Act (IIRIRA) of 1996. The act has several important provisions: (1) it significantly increases Border Patrol funding to combat undocumented immigration; (2) it bars undocumented immigrants caught in the United States from being legally admitted into the country for three or ten years afterwards, depending on the number of apprehensions; (3) it increases the number of deportable crimes (which now include many state misdemeanors such as burglaries and shoplifting); and (4) it reduces judicial oversight over deportation hearings. Although the purported targets of the deportable-crimes aspect of the immigration law are serious criminals, especially terrorists and drug dealers, many immigrants are deported for nonviolent misdemeanors. Other controversial aspects of this new law are the denial of federal social welfare programs to *legal* permanent residents and a requirement that sponsors of immigrants prove that they have an income equal to 125 percent of the poverty rate for the family plus the immigrant. (The former provision denying benefits to legal residents was overturned as a result of widespread protest.)

In addition, another trend has been increased funding for border agents along the border to deter undocumented immigration (DeSipio and de la Garza 1998). Beginning in 1993, the INS implemented a comprehensive

Topic Highlight: IIRIRA in Action

Gabriel Delgadillo was born in Coahuila, Mexico, and immigrated to the United States at the age of fifteen. The fifty-two-year-old legal Mexican immigrant, who had volunteered for service in Vietnam, was a farmworker in Bakersfield, California, site of many United Farm Workers activities and birthplace of the strike against grape growers in 1965.

One night in April 1999, Delgadillo returned permanently to Mexico, but he did not return voluntarily. He had been deported because earlier in 1999 he had sought disability benefits from the Veterans Administration. During the verification process a 1988 conviction for burglary was discovered. Even though Delgadillo had not been directly involved in the burglary, his car had been used, so Delgadillo had pleaded guilty to reduce the severity of the charges brought against him. Eleven years later, this conviction returned to haunt him because although his wife and children are U.S. citizens, he had never applied for U.S. citizenship.

Delgadillo thus was vulnerable to deportation under IIRIRA. The 1996 immigration law not only made many minor crimes deportable, but also applied retroactively to make *crimes committed before the law was enacted* deportable offenses. Stealing car stereos, shoplifting, domestic abuse, and other state misdemeanors are now classified as federal crimes, leaving many immigrants subject to deportation. Furthermore, the discretion that immigration judges once had in deportation cases is virtually eliminated under IIRIRA, so no judge had the discretion to overturn Delgadillo's deportation in light of his service to the country.

Only in July 2000 did the U.S. attorney general modify the regulations to give judges discretion in cases such as Delgadillo's. However, deported immigrants cannot have their cases reconsidered under this new interpretation. People like Delgadillo must suffer the consequences of immigration reform. If a Vietnam veteran is not good enough to remain in this country, then who is? (From Hartman 1999) ■

border plan that emphasized deterring illegal immigration by placing more agents along the border. As a consequence, the number of border patrol agents increased 127 percent between 1993 and 2000 (Meissner 2000). Presently, there are some nine thousand border patrol agents, although not all of them are stationed along the U.S.–Mexico border.

It is still unclear how Mexican immigrants will adjust, as they always do, to the latest immigration laws. The recent increase in **naturalization** rates may be one reaction. Given the loose and informal nature of immigration from Mexico, however, it is almost certain that many immigrants unaware of the new law's consequences will suffer deleterious effects. Similarly, it is unlikely that increased patrolling of the two thousand–mile U.S.–Mexico border will keep undocumented immigrants from entering the country. They will use crossing points not currently patrolled or will develop strategies that defeat the patrols.

■ Summary

Despite perceptions to the contrary, Mexican immigration has long been a part of the history of the Southwest. A combination of factors at the turn of the twentieth century led to the first large wave of Mexican immigration. The Mexican Revolution that began in 1910 created political, social, and economic forces that made everyday life in Mexico difficult. The transportation infrastructure built during the late nineteenth century enabled the movement of people north. In the United States, immigration legislation restricted Asian, and southern and eastern European immigration, reducing the availability of workers for the agricultural, railroad, and other labor-intensive industries. At the same time, the growth of agriculture and other labor-intensive industries increased the demand for laborers. Newly arrived Mexicans filled this void.

These early immigrants established social and employment networks throughout the United States that facilitated and maintained immigration for years to come, mostly from states in the north-central region of Mexico. Only the Great Depression put an end to the first wave of immigration.

The need for a temporary workforce during World War II precipitated a second wave of Mexican immigration through the Bracero Program. American agricultural and other industries profited from the availability of a cheap, abundant, and eager Mexican workforce, and the Bracero

Program was renewed continuously until 1964. In all, more than 4.5 million braceros found jobs in the United States.

From 1965 to 1990, the family-preference provisions of U.S. immigration laws and the prevailing economic conditions of both countries largely influenced Mexican legal immigration. The lack of limits on the number of family members who could immigrate made it possible for Mexico to receive more visas than the twenty thousand it was allocated. On the other hand, because Mexico has received only twenty thousand visas per year since 1976, the number of applicants who do not qualify for family-based visas has created a huge backlog of Mexicans waiting for visas.

The growing number of undocumented immigrants resulted in the Immigration Reform and Control Act of 1986. Although IRCA enabled 2.3 million Mexican immigrants to become permanent residents, the law did not succeed in halting undocumented immigration because it focused on employer sanctions, failing to recognize the complex push-pull motivations that impel Mexicans to leave their homeland. Continued fear about the impact of legal and illegal immigration culminated in the IIRIRA legislation of 1996 that makes it easier to deport immigrants for many minor crimes. Only four years after enactment have judges been given discretionary power over the application of this law.

Because the economic forces that drive Mexican immigration have not changed appreciably since 1965, attempts to limit legal and illegal immigration generally have failed. Ignoring the basic motivations that drive immigrants al norte, the legislation of the 1990s focused on punishing long-time legal residents by eliminating eligibility for social programs and deporting immigrants for minor crimes committed years ago.

Appendix: Human Capital Model of Migration

It is possible to illustrate formally how the relative economic opportunities in Mexico and the United States shape the composition of the immigrant population. First, assume that Mexicans base their decision to immigrate on the relative wages they can earn in Mexico and the United States. This is a realistic assumption, because the only major political event to cause large-scale migration was the Mexican Revolution of 1910–1920. All other waves of migration have been driven primarily by economic motivations.

Using a **human capital** model of wage determination, in which wages depend on the worker's level of education, it is possible to create a relationship between immigrants' wages in Mexico and wages in the United States. Economic theory postulates that individuals invest time, effort, and money to acquire skills (human capital) because employers reward these skills through higher wages. A major component of human capital is schooling. For this reason, economists find that education is a very good predictor of future wages.

If W represents the wage of a person, S the person's level of education (such as years of schooling, credits, or diploma), r the per-unit value of education, and m the minimum income earned by a person without any education ($S = 0$), the earnings function can be represented as

$$W = m + r \times S \qquad (1)$$

With this simple model of earnings attainment, the next step in the analysis speculates that immigrants decide to immigrate based on differences in wages in Mexico (W_M) and wages (net of migration costs) in the United States (W_{US}): an immigrant with S level of education recognizes that the American and Mexican labor markets have different structures; i.e., different values for r and m. In particular, it is well documented that every year of education has greater economic value in Mexico than in the United States, so $r_M > r_{US}$ (Borjas 1996). Furthermore, workers in the United States receive higher minimum wages than workers in Mexico, so $m_{US} > m_M$. As a consequence of these differences, the wages in Mexico for a person can be calculated using

$$W_M = m_M + r_M \times S \qquad (2)$$

The U.S. wage-determination equation is not exactly analogous to the Mexican wage function in (2). Immigration entails many costs, such as leaving your family and friends, the actual transportation costs, the costs of learning a new language, culture shock, and other monetary and non-monetary costs. Assume that these costs can be translated into dollar figures and C denotes the full cost of migration. These costs must be subtracted from earnings in the United States, W_{US}^*, so that *net U.S. wages* are $W_{US} = W_{US}^* - C$. Therefore, a Mexican immigrant with S years of education in the United States will earn

$$W_{US} = m_{US} - C + r_{US} \times S \qquad (3)$$

A person who decides that net wages are greater in the United States than in Mexico ($W_{US} > W_M$) will immigrate. On the other hand, a person for whom the opposite is true will choose to stay in Mexico. Individuals whose net wages are equal in both countries will be indifferent between migrating to the United States and remaining in Mexico.

Although these may seem to be obvious conclusions, the model can also be used to predict which persons stay in Mexico and which emigrate. In order to better illustrate this, it is useful to interpret S as a measure of education relative to the average level of schooling in Mexico. In other words, given that the average years of education (S_{avg}) in Mexico is ten, then $S = 0$ represents an immigrant with the same level of education as the average Mexican, $S = -2$ an immigrant with only eight years of education, and so on.

Figure 5 graphs wage equations (2) and (3), with the assumption that $m_{US} - C > m_M$, or that migration costs are such that a Mexican with an average level of education does not view these costs as too high to immigrate. On the vertical axis are wages, which increase with higher levels of schooling. In the case where $S = 0$, wages in the United States are $m_{US} - C$ and wages in Mexico are m_M, which are shown as the two vertical intercepts. Since $r_M > r_{US}$, the earnings function in Mexico is *steeper* than the American earnings function, which implies that wages increase more in Mexico than in the United States for every additional year of relative education.

The two earnings functions cross at S^*. The importance of figure 5 becomes apparent when it is recognized that for every level of schooling greater than S^*, wages are always greater in Mexico, and for schooling levels lower than S^*, earnings are higher in the United States. In this case S^* is greater than S_{avg}, the average education of Mexicans. In other words, this model predicts that as long as net U.S. wages are greater than wages in Mexico, immigrants with education levels ranging from below average to somewhat above average will benefit from immigration. However, Mexicans with a college degree are very unlikely to migrate according to this model.

In 1990, the average years of education of recent Mexican immigrants was around eight years, whereas the average years of schooling in Mexico was slightly less than seven (Secretaría de Educación Pública 1998). This suggests that the graphical model does indeed partly capture the factors behind who leaves and who stays in Mexico.

The implication from the immigration model is this: those who migrate

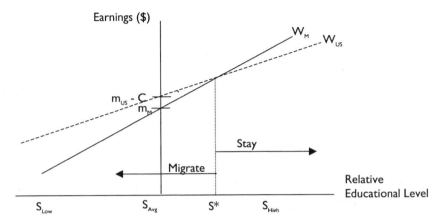

Figure 5. Economic factors driving the decision to immigrate.

are different from the populations in both the home and host countries. Mexican immigrants in the United States have education levels just slightly higher than the average person in Mexico. Because the American labor market rewards less-educated workers much better than the Mexican labor market does, Mexicans with near-average education levels are better off moving to the United States. Those who choose to migrate are not a random draw from the Mexican population, but rather are "self-selected" for immigration based on specific characteristics (low education and low migration costs).

Application—Tougher Immigration Policies

One result of the low average levels of schooling in the immigrant stream has been an attack on Mexican immigrants as underskilled, uneducated, uncultured, and hence a social problem and a liability for the health, education, and welfare system. In sum, they are seen and portrayed as undesirable. One way to approach this perceived problem is to establish barriers that impede their legal and illegal immigration, with the hope that doing so will reduce the undesirable element within the immigrant flow. Since the graphical model incorporates these barriers as higher migration costs, C, it is possible to examine the consequences of increasing the cost of immigration, say, $C^* > C$.

Higher costs come into play in the model through the fact that they shift the U.S. earnings function down. As C^* is greater than C, this means the vertical intercept $m_{US} - C^*$ is at a lower point on the vertical axis than was the previous intercept, $m_{US} - C$. However, this reduces the incentive to immigrate by the same amount *for everyone*. To see this, examine the migration decision of the person with S^* level of education. It was established that given the previous migration costs of C, a person with S^* education is indifferent about whether to migrate. With the higher migration costs of C^*, this person now discovers that it is not worthwhile to immigrate and stays in Mexico. Thus the point at which a person becomes indifferent about migrating or staying is now at a level of education lower than S^*.

Although the lessened incentive to immigrate reduces the number of people who migrate (the flow), it also has another effect. Because everyone faces the higher cost of immigrating, only those with low levels of education still benefit economically from immigrating. The average education of the immigrant population, therefore, is now lower as a consequence of tougher immigration policies! In other words, if the goal of tougher immigration policies is to "improve" the quality (as measured by education) of immigrants, then these policies actually accomplish the opposite. The education level of individual immigrants does not decrease, rather the average education level of the immigrant population decreases, because more educated immigrants now choose to stay in Mexico.

■ Discussion Questions

1. How recent is immigration from Mexico?

2. How did pre-1964 immigration influence more recent immigration?

3. Why was the Bracero Program initially retained much longer than intended, and then terminated in the 1960s?

4. How did the Immigration and Nationality Act of 1965 affect immigration from Mexico?

5. Why did IRCA fail to reduce undocumented immigration over the long term?

6. What are some possible explanations for the harshness of IIRIRA as exemplified by the Topic Highlight?

◼ Suggested Readings

Annerino, John. 1999. *Dead in Their Tracks: Crossing America's Desert Borderlands*. New York: Four Walls Eight Windows.

DeFreitas, Gregory. 1991. *Inequality at Work: Hispanics in the U.S. Labor Force*. New York: Oxford University Press.

Meier, Matt S., and Feliciano Ribera. 1993. *Mexican Americans/American Mexicans*. New York: Hill and Wang.

Monroy, Douglas. 1999. *Rebirth: Mexican Los Angeles from the Great Migration and the Great Depression*. Berkeley: University of California Press.

Rothenberg, Daniel. 1998. *With These Hands*. New York: Harcourt Brace.

Vargas, Zaragosa. 1993. *Proletarians of the North: A History of Mexican Industrial Workers in Detroit and the Midwest, 1917–1933*. Berkeley: University of California Press.

3

Aquí Estamos

MEXICAN IMMIGRANTS IN THE UNITED STATES TODAY

Héctor González is a team leader at a national company that manufactures plastic dishes in Southern California. His rise through the company—from packer of dishes, to materials handler, to operator, to supervisor, and finally to team leader—parallels his experience as a Mexican immigrant in the United States. In search of employment, he entered the United States using false documents at the age of seventeen. With the help of family and friends, he found jobs picking oranges, lemons, and grapes in the San Joaquin Valley in California. Later, due to discrimination by a new manager, he was fired from his job as a busboy in the desert town of Baker, California, where he had worked for one year. Although he earned the minimum wage, his growing work experience made it possible for him to find jobs in Southern California's manufacturing and restaurant industries. By the time he began working for his current employer in 1980, he had learned English. His superiors recognized his ability and work ethic, and he began his rise within the company soon thereafter. The economic security he was gaining was soon followed by marriage, children, homeownership, then the attainment of legal status, and finally by American citizenship. González's story is not unique—his story is repeated among thousands of other Mexican immigrants now living in the United States.

Mexican immigration is an important topic with which to begin an examination of Mexican Americans in the U.S. economy. In some respects, the popular perception of Mexican Americans is based on Mexican immigrants. Therefore, if an economic portrait of Mexican Americans is to be built, the natural starting point is to develop a more enlightened understanding of Mexican immigrants. Doing so makes it easier to challenge long-held notions about who Mexican Americans are and to promote their acceptance as Americans.

This chapter focuses on current topics in immigration to build on the theme that Mexican Americans strive for *buenos días*. The goal is to present a realistic, and generally positive, portrait of Mexicans and Mexican Americans. Having provided a foundation and basic understanding of Mexican immigration in chapter 2, this chapter examines various topics that currently make headlines and help shape public perceptions of Mexican Americans. The rest of the chapter contains an economic and demographic profile of immigrants, as well as a discussion of immigrant settlement patterns, the economic **assimilation** of immigrants, the economic impact of immigration, **undocumented immigration,** and **naturalization.**

■ Economic and Demographic Profile of Mexican Immigrants

Table 2 shows the most recent data available on selected socioeconomic and demographic characteristics of Mexican immigrants. For poverty, income, and welfare programs, the information applies to 1998; all other statistics pertain to 1999. In all, there are more than 7.2 million Mexican immigrants in the United States, 45 percent of whom are female.

Mexican immigrants are a very young population. Nearly half (46.5 percent) of all immigrants are between the ages of nineteen and thirty-five, 13.2 percent are eighteen years or younger, and only 4.8 percent are older than sixty-five. In contrast, non-Mexican immigrants are more concentrated in the older age categories. Gender does not affect the age composition of Mexican immigrants, although there are slightly more elderly Mexican women than men, a finding consistent with the U.S. population as a whole.

The youthfulness of the Mexican immigrant population has important educational and health implications. As most immigrants are raised in Spanish-speaking households, U.S. schools face the challenge of educating children who do not have the background that prepares them for the standard curriculum. Schools must be prepared to implement a curriculum that is rigorous yet relevant to these students' experience through means such as providing culturally competent teachers (Delgado Bernal 1998). In terms of health policy, attention needs to be given to prenatal health and childhood diseases, especially transmittable diseases such as tuberculosis (Abraído-Lanza et al. 1999; González-Baker 1996). On the other hand, young people are generally healthier than older people, so the

Table 2 Selected Characteristics of Immigrants by Gender, March 1999

	MEXICAN IMMIGRANTS			NON-MEXICAN IMMIGRANTS		
	Total	Male	Female	Total	Male	Female
POPULATION (IN 1,000s)	7,240	3,984	3,256	19,247	9,146	10,101
AGE						
0–10	4.8%	5.0%	4.5%	3.1%	2.9%	3.2%
11–18	8.4%	9.1%	7.6%	6.1%	6.8%	5.4%
19–25	16.8%	17.8%	15.6%	9.6%	10.2%	9.1%
26–35	29.7%	29.6%	29.7%	21.3%	22.6%	20.2%
36–55	29.9%	29.6%	30.3%	36.8%	37.0%	36.6%
56–65	5.7%	5.0%	6.5%	10.3%	9.2%	11.2%
66+	4.8%	3.9%	5.9%	12.9%	11.3%	14.3%
HIGHEST GRADE COMPLETED (25 YEARS OR OLDER)						
No schooling	8.1%	8.3%	7.9%	5.5%	5.6%	5.3%
1–8 grades	40.9%	40.5%	41.5%	12.7%	11.9%	13.4%
9–11 grades	21.1%	21.4%	20.8%	11.3%	11.8%	10.8%
High school diploma	19.0%	19.5%	18.2%	23.6%	21.9%	25.1%
Some college (no bachelor's)	7.8%	7.2%	8.5%	18.9%	17.9%	19.8%
Bachelor's degree	2.2%	2.0%	2.5%	17.7%	17.5%	17.9%
Master's degree or higher	1.0%	1.2%	0.7%	10.4%	13.4%	7.6%
LABOR FORCE STATUS (15 YEARS OR OLDER AND NOT IN ARMED FORCES)						
Employed	62.8%	80.7%	41.0%	61.2%	70.9%	52.3%
Umemployed	4.5%	4.5%	4.5%	3.2%	3.5%	2.9%
Not in labor force	32.7%	14.8%	54.5%	35.7%	25.5%	44.8%
INCOME, 1998						
$0–$2,500	33.2%	19.8%	49.6%	24.6%	17.7%	30.9%
$2,501–$9,999	19.4%	16.4%	23.1%	17.1%	11.9%	21.9%
$10,000–$19,999	28.0%	34.6%	19.9%	20.2%	20.7%	19.8%
$20,000–$34,999	14.4%	21.6%	5.7%	17.2%	19.4%	15.2%
$35,000–$49,999	2.9%	4.5%	1.1%	8.7%	11.7%	6.0%
$50,000+	2.1%	3.2%	0.7%	12.1%	18.6%	6.2%
POVERTY AND WELFARE PARTICIPATION, 1998						
In poverty	28.5%	25.8%	31.8%	14.1%	11.9%	16.1%
Receiving public assistance	2.4%	0.3%	4.9%	1.7%	0.7%	2.5%
Receiving food stamps	11.7%	7.9%	19.3%	6.2%	3.5%	10.0%
Receiving AFDC	3.9%	0.5%	10.7%	1.9%	0.4%	4.1%

Source: Author's weighted tabulations from the March 1999 Current Population Survey.

youthfulness of the population also results in a healthier population. As a consequence of this, emphasis on prevention would most likely be a sound strategy.

The education figures in table 2 are collected only for those twenty-five years and older, as this group is most likely to have completed their education. These figures show that the educational attainment of Mexican immigrants is concentrated on the low end of the education distribution. More than 70 percent of Mexican immigrants do not have a high-school diploma, and only 3.2 percent have a bachelor's or higher degree. Gender does not have a significant effect on educational attainment. In contrast, non-Mexican immigrants are more likely to have at least a high-school diploma. In fact, nearly half of non-Mexican immigrants have some kind of college experience, compared to 11 percent of Mexican immigrants.

The average Mexican immigrant has approximately nine years of education, meaning that he or she left school around the age of fourteen or fifteen. Given this low level of basic education, it is difficult for the average teenage Mexican immigrant to make a smooth transition into American schools. Investment in education is most likely to involve English or civics courses that are particularly beneficial in the labor market or are required for citizenship.

On the other hand, the immigrant children who are educated in the United States are capable of performing just as well as native Mexican American children, although their success is affected by their age at arrival. Immigrants who arrive at or near the start of primary school are likely to perform just as well as Mexican Americans, but immigrants who arrive at older ages will attain fewer and fewer years of education (A. González 2000). U.S.–born children of Mexican immigrants must overcome several difficulties associated with growing up in a household that is unfamiliar with the education system and may lack knowledge about the economic benefits associated with postsecondary education. In addition, the parents' inability to help their children with schoolwork is a detriment to the educational development of many Mexican American children. These, along with other factors, impact the education of Mexican immigrants and Mexican Americans. Schools must be prepared to meet the needs of immigrant children, especially with regard to language, curriculum, and social integration. Issues of education for Mexican Americans and Mexican immigrants are discussed in chapter 4.

Income and Poverty

Figure 6 shows the distribution of income by citizenship status among Mexican immigrants who reported income for 1998. Although time in the United States is a significant factor in the growth of wages—and the majority of immigrants arrived in the past fifteen to twenty years—the earnings of Mexican immigrants are still concentrated in the lower end of the income distribution, regardless of citizenship status. More than 70 percent of Mexican immigrants earned less than $20,000 per year in 1998. At the other extreme, less than 5 percent of immigrants earn $50,000 or more.

Considering that many workers support family and non-family members, the large preponderance of low-income workers can be expected to result in large numbers of Mexican immigrants living in poverty. **Poverty status** is determined by comparing total family income to family size. For example, in 1998, the poverty level for a sixty-five-year-old person living alone was $8,500, whereas for a family of four an income of $16,500 was the poverty cutoff (U.S. Bureau of the Census 1999).

Using this formal definition of poverty, 28.5 percent of all Mexican immigrants lived below the poverty line in 1998, compared to 14.1 percent of non-Mexican immigrants (see table 2). Furthermore, Mexican men (25.8 percent) are 6 percentage points less likely to live in poverty than women (31.8 percent).

The higher incidence of poverty among Mexican immigrants is in part a consequence of various socioeconomic factors, including lower education levels. Another factor is that recent arrivals are likely to begin at the bottom of the economic ladder, but with increasing time in the United States, immigrants tend to improve their economic situation.

Figure 7 shows the percentage of immigrants living in poverty in 1998, grouped by decade of arrival as well as Mexican/non-Mexican and naturalized citizen/noncitizen status. One clear pattern is that a higher percentage of recently arrived immigrants are living in poverty. For example, 21 percent of noncitizen Mexican immigrants who arrived before 1970 were living in poverty, compared to 39 percent of those who arrived in the 1990s. One likely explanation for this general outcome is that recently arrived immigrants are younger and have less U.S. work experience.

Another pattern evident in figure 7 is that Mexican immigrants tend to have a higher incidence of poverty than non-Mexicans. For example,

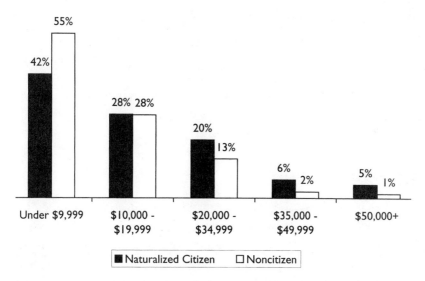

■ Figure 6. Income distribution of Mexican immigrants by citizenship status, 1998. (Source: Author's weighted tabulations from the March 1999 Current Population Survey)

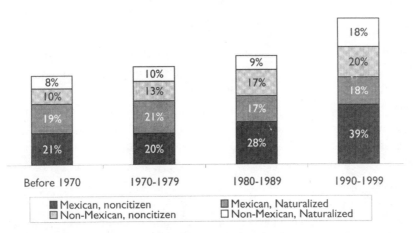

■ Figure 7. Percentage of immigrants living in poverty in 1998, by year of arrival. (Source: Author's weighted tabulations from the March 1999 Current Population Survey)

28 percent of noncitizen Mexicans who arrived in the 1980s were in poverty in 1998, compared to 17 percent of noncitizen non-Mexicans. In contrast, the poverty rates for naturalized Mexican Americans are lower than for noncitizen Mexican U.S. residents and comparable to those for non-Mexicans. For example, non-Mexicans arriving after 1990 have poverty

rates of 18 to 20 percent for citizens and noncitizens respectively, compared to a rate of 18 percent for naturalized Mexican Americans.

Chapter 5 examines in detail the implications of poverty for welfare participation, but table 2 shows that in general Mexican immigrants make less use of such programs than would be expected given their high poverty rates. Evidence suggests, however, that recently arrived immigrants are more likely to use welfare (Borjas and Trejo 1991).

Settlement Patterns

Like Italians, Chinese, and other large national-origin groups in the United States, Mexicans tend to live in **enclaves**, or neighborhoods where others from the same country live. The major factors behind settlement decisions are a past history of settlement in the region by other Mexicans, job and housing conditions, and more generally, the cultural makeup of a particular enclave (A. González 1998). Other demographic characteristics influencing settlement decisions include marital status, age, education, citizenship status, and **international migration networks** (Bartel 1989; Massey 1999).

International migration networks play a role in the initial settlement decision of immigrants. Due to unfamiliarity with the new country, recent arrivals often rely on previous immigrants to help them navigate the various institutions. Relatives or friends of immigrants in the United States provide not only information about jobs but also temporary housing and other types of support. Since new arrivals are not familiar with most aspects of American culture, migration networks ease the transition by providing information quickly and efficiently. With time, however, immigrants learn many aspects of American society, and as a consequence their reliance on and ties to immigrant enclaves decline.

The settlement patterns of immigrants do not remain static, however. Although the presence of other immigrants and social networks continues to play a significant role in the settlement process, with increased time in the United States immigrants are more likely to move out of enclaves and into outlying regions and areas far from enclaves (Funkhouser 1995). Internal migration (that is, movement and settlement within the United States) is influenced not only by the above-mentioned demographic variables, but also by the process of assimilation, in which immigrants reduce their reliance on enclaves, as well as by the relative economic opportunities available in different cities. During the initial twenty years of U.S. resi-

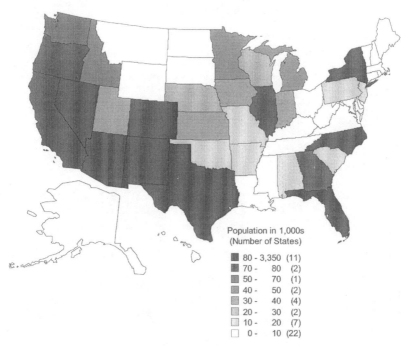

Population in 1,000s
(Number of States)

80 - 3,350	(11)
70 - 80	(2)
50 - 70	(1)
40 - 50	(2)
30 - 40	(4)
20 - 30	(2)
10 - 20	(7)
0 - 10	(22)

Figure 8. Mexican immigrants by state of residence (including Washington, D.C.), March 1999. Excludes persons living in group quarters. The numbers in parentheses in the key indicate the number of states in each population category. (Source: Author's weighted tabulations from the March 1999 Current Population Survey)

dence, immigrants are likely to live with other immigrants. After twenty years, however, residential assimilation is statistically more likely.

Figure 8 shows the distribution of the 7.2 million Mexican immigrants across the United States in March 1999. The states of residence for the overwhelming majority of Mexican immigrants are California and Texas, with more than 75 percent of all immigrants living in these states. Nearly 90 percent of all Mexican immigrants lived in ten states (in order of population): California, Texas, Illinois, Arizona, New York, Oregon, Florida, Nevada, Colorado, and New Mexico. Within these states, immigrants are more likely to live in urban than rural areas, and within these urban areas, to reside in neighborhoods comprised mostly of Mexicans or Mexican Americans (A. González 1998).

Table 3 shows the largest Mexican immigrant enclaves in 1980 and 1990. In 1990, the top five metropolitan areas of residence were Los Angeles, San Francisco, Chicago, Houston, and Dallas. The growth in immigrant population over the ten years is substantial, as exemplified by the

Table 3 Primary and Secondary Mexican Immigrant Enclaves, 1980 and 1990

Primary Enclave[1]	1980	1990	Secondary Enclave[1]	1980	1990
Los Angeles, Calif.	937,500	1,848,700	Odessa, Tex.	8,500	19,100
San Francisco, Calif.	176,700	369,900	Las Vegas, Nev.	5,500	18,800
Chicago, Ill.	172,900	279,200	Portland, Ore.	—[4]	17,900
Houston, Tex.	95,600	198,100	Yuma, Ariz.	—[4]	17,200
Dallas, Tex.	58,200	160,100	Tampa, Fla.	—[4]	16,300
Fresno, Calif.	68,200	148,000	Denver, Colo.	13,300	—[3]
El Paso, Tex.	85,500	140,100	Albuquerque, N. Mex.	5,200	12,200
McAllen, Tex.	87,300	135,300	Atlanta, Ga.	—[4]	10,200
Phoenix, Ariz.	40,900	106,500	Oklahoma City, Okla.	—[4]	10,000
San Antonio, Tex.	63,600	95,800	Yuba City, Calif.	—[4]	9,800
New York, N.Y.	—[2]	53,000	Washington, D.C.	—[4]	9,800
Denver, Colo.	—[2]	26,400	New York, N.Y.	9,800	—[3]
Yakima, Wash.	—[2]	23,500	Kansas City, Mo./Kans.	—[4]	8,400
Miami, Fla.	—[4]	20,400	Yakima, Wash.	8,400	—[3]
			Milwaukee, Wisc.	—[4]	7,300
			Detroit, Mich.	7,600	7,300
			Seattle, Wash.	—[4]	6,300
			Orlando, Fla.	—[4]	5,700
			Reno, Nev.	—[4]	5,200
			Salt Lake City, Utah	—[4]	5,000

Source: Funkhouser (1995).
[1]Primary enclaves are defined as areas with more than 20,000 immigrants in nearby adjoining Metropolitan Statistical Areas. Secondary enclaves are areas with 5,000 to 20,000 immigrants in adjoining Metropolitan Statistical Areas. Enclaves are listed in order of 1990 population.
[2]Secondary enclave in 1980.
[3]Primary enclave in 1990.
[4]Not an enclave.

near doubling of the immigrant population in Los Angeles, from 0.9 to 1.8 million. Furthermore, whereas ten primary and seven secondary enclaves existed in 1980, fourteen primary and seventeen secondary enclaves existed in 1990. Clearly, many cities grew in immigrant population over these ten years to reach enclave status. Note also that the new secondary enclaves are located in areas not traditionally associated with Mexican settlement, such as Salt Lake City and Atlanta. It is likely that new international migration networks are being created in these new enclaves, and the Mexican population in these areas can be expected to continue increasing.

■ Wage Assimilation

The previous sections of this chapter have revealed an economically vulnerable population. Yet, the statistics fail to capture the economic assimilation of immigrants into the U.S. labor markets. Because table 2 and figure 6 combine recently arrived with more experienced immigrants, it is not possible to examine whether the wages of immigrants improve simply as a consequence of **wage assimilation,** defined as wage parity with comparable U.S.–born workers.

Because the majority of Mexican immigrants enter the U.S. labor market with limited knowledge and job skills, their initial wages are typically lower than those of comparable U.S.–born workers (Borjas 1994; Chiswick 1978). As immigrants acquire information about American employers and jobs, and increase their English skills and other valuable **human capital,** they may be able to find jobs better suited to their qualifications and lifestyles. Over time, then, in theory their wages might approach the wages of natives. Therefore, an interesting question to examine is whether immigrants do assimilate economically.

Immigrants and natives typically differ in human capital endowments, such as work experience, marital status, region of residence, English ability, and education. These differences partially explain the lower wages of immigrants, so only after adjusting for them is it possible to isolate and measure the assimilation effect. Using years of residence as a measure of assimilation, Chiswick (1978) found that newly arrived Mexican immigrants did indeed earn less than U.S.–born natives, but that after ten to fifteen years their earnings matched those of natives, and soon thereafter actually surpassed natives' wages. Several other studies have also found evidence of economic assimilation (Funkhouser and Trejo 1995; LaLonde and Topel 1992; Reimers 1997).

More recent studies, however, shed doubt on the extent of wage assimilation. One of the more influential studies argues that immigrants reach wage parity with *comparable* natives after twenty or so years in the United States, but then begin to earn relatively less (Borjas 1996). In other words, whereas immigrants who arrived in the 1970s and before earn pretty much the same as demographically similar natives, immigrants who arrived in the 1980s are predicted to earn about 10 percent less than comparable natives. In essence, the conclusion is that the prospects for full wage assimilation are limited for recent arrivals but are better for pre-1980 immigrants.

Even if the bleakest conclusions are true, immigrants still make significant gains over the course of their U.S. employment experience. When immigrants who arrived in the 1980s first entered the job market, they earned 50 percent less than native non-Hispanic whites (Borjas 1996). The experience they acquired after as little as ten years reduced the wage gap to only 10 to 15 percent. In other words, even though immigrants earned 50 cents on the dollar when they first started working, their earnings deficit was reduced until they earned 85 to 90 cents to the native worker's dollar with as little as ten years of U.S. residence and work experience. Over the next ten years, the relative wages of Mexican immigrants continued to improve.

The implication from these studies is that the labor market experiences of immigrants are dynamic rather than stable, and they improve with length of residence in the United States. Immigrants take advantage of opportunities to advance economically. Looking at the poverty rates in figure 7, therefore, it is possible to argue that earlier waves of immigrants have had a greater amount of time to economically assimilate. Even if immigrants do not achieve full wage parity, they eliminate most or all of the wage gap between themselves and native workers. The evidence for wage assimilation among Mexican immigrants is more positive than bleak.

■ Economic Impact of Immigration

In 1994, Jesse Laguna wrote in the *Los Angeles Times* that "the state of California can no longer be the Department of Health, Education and Welfare for the rest of the world." He stated that he and many other Hispanics supported Proposition 187—which was intended to deny educational and social services to undocumented immigrants—because immigrants were "hollering for freebies." The argument that immigrants come to the United States primarily to receive social services, and that they abuse these services, is a common one among those who support restrictive immigration policies such as Proposition 187. A second common anti-immigration argument is the so-called **displacement effect,** which argues that immigrants take jobs away from or reduce the wages of native workers. Even though these two arguments contradict each other, they share a common thread that immigrants have a negative impact on the U.S. economy (Funkhouser 1996).

Several attempts have been made to assess the economic impact of immigrants (Funkhouser 1996; Smith and Edmonston 1997). Unfortunately, the first conclusion reached is that it is *impossible* to measure the full impact of immigration on the trillion-dollar U.S. economy, partly because of its sheer size. A strategy used by researchers, therefore, is to examine the impact of immigration on specific segments of the economy, such as labor markets (specifically employment and wages) and utilization of government services.

The majority of studies examine the fiscal impact of immigrants by comparing the taxes paid and services received by immigrants. One of the studies most often cited by anti-immigration supporters totaled particular taxes paid by immigrants and the costs of providing various services to conclude that immigrants cost taxpayers nearly $44 billion in 1992. The consensus among the majority of researchers was that this study had many flaws, however, including inaccurate population, tax, and cost estimates. Another group of researchers remedied these shortcomings by using more precise estimates of the undocumented population, as well as improved tax and cost figures, and concluded that all Mexican immigration *benefited* natives by the amount of $31 billion in 1992 (Funkhouser 1996).

Both studies fall short of providing the necessary information to make reasonable policy decisions, however. Even if it were possible to examine all sectors of the economy, the social, noneconomic impact is still ignored. Since immigrants affect U.S. society in many ways other than economically, it would be a mistake to base policy decisions solely on economic estimates.

Moreover, it is difficult to estimate the exact fiscal impact because it is impossible to measure the full utilization of services as well as the total taxes paid by immigrants. In addition, both studies limit their analysis to one year, 1992, and do not consider the future impact of immigration. This is important given the likelihood that young immigrant workers will help sustain programs such as Social Security at a time when the American workforce is aging (Hayes-Bautista 1993).

More importantly, however, both studies examine what immigrants paid and what they received, not *the fiscal impact* on public finances. To better assess the fiscal impact of immigrants, it is necessary to consider the present and future impact of immigration on all segments of society, including households, employers and employees, consumers, government, and landlords. For example, to examine how immigration affects the labor market outcomes of natives, it is necessary to consider the current and future net effect on earnings and employment to both native workers and employers; the current and future taxes paid by all natives directly and indirectly; the future net effect on the national product; and the future net effect on the nonworking population in terms of lower prices for goods, Social Security payments, and so on.

In the case of the impact on native wages and employment, the majority of studies find that immigrants do not have an overall displacement effect on the labor market outcomes of natives (Funkhouser 1996). In the studies where an effect is found, there is a small negative impact on both employment and wages of similar workers (low-skilled native workers, similarly educated Mexican Americans). However, the displacement argument made by anti-immigration supporters ignores the positive effect on other types of workers, such as females or more educated workers, and the positive employment effects caused by greater consumption of consumer products by immigrants. For the displacement theory to be true, the following conditions must hold: (1) the number of jobs must be fixed; (2) immigrants must substitute for natives in production; and (3) immigrants must be willing to work for lower wages than equally productive natives. Economists find none of these conditions is met in theory or in practice.

The accusation made by Jesse Laguna that immigrants are "hollering" for welfare and social service benefits is exaggerated. Although it is true that recent immigrants are more likely than previous immigrants to receive some type of public assistance, it is also the case that natives are more likely than immigrants of identical characteristics to use any type of social welfare (Borjas and Trejo 1991; Smith and Edmonston 1997). Because only permanent residents and citizens are eligible for public assistance programs, undocumented immigrants, who were the target of California's Proposition 187, are not likely to be a burden in this regard.

Statistics indicate that the programs used by a significant (more than 5 percent) percentage of Mexican immigrants are Medicaid (10.7 percent of all Mexicans) and Food Stamps (11.7 percent of Mexican households). Immigrants use public medical funds as a last resort, usually in emergencies (often the result of illnesses that have gone untreated) or for childbirth. Therefore, Laguna's statement is not supported by statistics.

One of the largest areas of spending on immigrants is education. In addition to schooling, immigrant children require some English-language instruction and may require more time to complete their education because they are more likely to be held back (Delgado Bernal 1998; Vernez,

Abrahamse, and Quigley 1996). The growing number of immigrant children prompts some to argue that children of undocumented immigrants be denied a free public education. California and Texas crafted legislation with this goal specifically in mind (Delgado Bernal 1998). On the other hand, given that these children are very likely to remain in and eventually work in the United States, it is in our national interest to encourage all immigrant students to attain as much education as possible (A. González 2000). Educated workers are more likely to earn higher wages, to be promoted, to suffer shorter spells of unemployment, and to experience other positive labor market outcomes. The net effect is that educated Mexican immigrants will contribute more in taxes over their lifetime than the cost of their education (A. González 2000).

Another argument made by anti-immigration groups is that the federal government should reimburse states with a large number of immigrants for the costs of services provided to legal and undocumented immigrants. California and Florida were two states that filed federal lawsuits to recoup money spent on educating, imprisoning, and providing other services to immigrants (Funkhouser 1996). They argued that the federal government is responsible for immigration policy and receives the majority of immigrant taxes, but the states bear the brunt of costs for providing health care, education, and other services to immigrants, and therefore, immigrant-receiving states should receive federal compensation. Although these lawsuits generated a great deal of attention, they were unsuccessful. As Funkhouser (1996) pointed out, it is unclear that federal compensation is the correct policy response. First of all, there is no precedent for this type of redistribution of income. Second, many individuals within the states benefit, including consumers, landlords, and employers. As a consequence, a more equitable policy would be to transfer revenue from those who benefit to those who lose within the same state.

Undocumented Immigrants

Of the estimated 5 million undocumented immigrants in 1997, approximately 2.7 million (54 percent) are from Mexico, and some 150,000 enter the United States per year (INS 1999b). After Mexico, the most common countries of origin for undocumented immigrants are El Salvador, Guatemala, and Canada. The INS (1997) classifies undocumented immigrants as either **Overstayers** or EWIs (for **entry without inspection**). Overstayers are immigrants who remain in the United States illegally after their student, tourist, work, or other visa has expired. Entry without inspection refers to immigrants who have not been inspected for entry into the United States at any port of entry. In other words, these are immigrants who were smuggled across the border by **coyotes** or were able to cross illegally on their own.

Undocumented Mexican immigrants are more likely to be EWIS than overstayers. Undocumented immigrants are similar in many ways to other Mexican immigrants. Yet because they are in the country illegally, they are more susceptible to discrimination and abuse and have more difficulty integrating into society (Borjas 1991; Massey 1987; Rothenberg 1998).

Despite perceptions to the contrary, undocumented immigration is nothing new (see chapter 2). The first undocumented immigrants to the Southwest were the Spanish conquistadors who settled Texas, New Mexico, and California. After Mexico gained its independence, the next stream of undocumented immigrants (or "aliens" in the official federal terminology) were Americans from the Midwest and East Coast. In the 1820s and 1830s, many Anglos crossed into Texas to settle on the fertile plains. The Mexican government was largely unsuccessful in turning back the stream of undocumented American immigrants.

Despite the establishment of a new political boundary separating Mexico and the United States after the U.S.–Mexico War, the history and culture of the Southwest made it impossible to separate people of Mexican descent on both sides of the border. As a consequence, Mexicans crossed the border frequently, either to visit relatives short distances away "on the other side" or to seek employment. Little attention was paid to the legal status of Mexican immigrants prior to 1900. In fact, the history of discrimination against American-born Mexicans all but negated the value of citizenship or legal status. Mexican Americans were no better than Mexicans, even if their families had lived in the Southwest for generations.

When the **Bracero** Program was widened in scope during the mid-1950s, the economic incentive to work in the United States became greater than ever for Mexicans. Since many could attain bracero status once they found employment in the United States, it was generally more convenient for Mexicans to cross the border illegally than to do the necessary paperwork for a visa or work permit. As the number of undocumented immigrants grew throughout the 1950s, the United States responded with several mass legalizations. With the end of the Bracero Program in 1964, the mechanism that had reduced undocumented immigration disappeared. It is not surprising then, that the number of undocumented immigrants increased to between 2.5 and 3.5 million by the 1980s. Perceived as the source of various social ills from unemployment to crime to the decline of U.S. industrial might, undocumented immigration became a target of federal law, beginning with IRCA (the **Immigration Reform and Control Act**) in 1986. As chapter 2 showed, IRCA was largely unsuccessful in reducing undocumented immigration.

Information that is known about current undocumented immigrants shows that, contrary to common belief, they are not predominantly lone young men working in agriculture (Massey 1987; Smith and Edmonston 1997). Demographic studies of undocumented immigrants from rural Mexican towns reveal that only slightly more than half are men; many women come illegally into the United States as well (Massey 1987). In addition, only about 30 percent of undocumented immigrants are between the ages of fifteen and twenty-four. Rather than being alone in this country, many live with relatives. In fact, researchers have found that immigrants are more likely to attempt to enter illegally if they have family members in the United States. Another factor is previous experience; Mexicans who have crossed the border illegally in the past are more likely to attempt to cross the border than are similar Mexicans (Hanson and Spilimbergo 1999).

Due partly to their immigration status, undocumented immigrants tend to be seasonal or temporary U.S. residents, unless they have strong ties to the United States such as their spouse and children living here. Seasonal jobs are common in the construction, restaurant, and agricultural industries. The seasonal and temporary nature of such employment results in immigrants making repeated border crossings within years, and sometimes months, of the previous trip.

As discussed in chapter 2, this situation corresponds to the sojourner phase of immigration. Another characteristic of the sojourner phase is that many immigrants save much of the money earned in the United States and remit it to their families in Mexico. It has been estimated that the sending communities in Mexico benefit greatly from the money earned abroad. In many cases, money earned in the United States revitalizes poor or dying communities as families are able to build and improve their homes, have more food, and generally increase their standard of living (Rothenberg 1998).

Although immigrants (both undocumented and legal) benefit from working in the United States, concerns and accusations of widespread abuse and discrimination against immigrants, particularly undocumented immigrants, persist. Vernon Briggs states, " '[A] shadow labor force' has evolved whose presence is often felt but seldom seen. It is composed of a body of workers who are totally dependent upon the terms of employment set by employers. Such a situation is ripe for exploitation. . . . [Undocumented workers are] frequently victimized by employers who know of their vulnerability" (Massey 1987, 237).

Because undocumented workers fear being discovered, they may be less likely to report mistreatment. In addition, as participants in the black labor market, they may face worse working conditions and wages than legal immigrants or natives do. For example, a common anecdote tells of employers calling the INS to deport undocumented workers on payday. Prior to 1986, employers were not legally liable for hiring undocumented workers, so such situations may well have occurred. Since the passage of IRCA, however, employers who "knowingly" hire undocumented workers are subject to fines and other legal **employer sanctions,** so it is unlikely they would systematically subject themselves to possible investigation by making frequent phone calls to the INS.

The majority of studies find that, on average, undocumented immigrants do earn less than legal immigrants. This does not necessarily mean that undocumented immigrants are exploited, however. They are also younger than legal immigrants, tend to speak less English, and have less experience in the United States because of their seasonal migration patterns. After taking these differences into consideration, undocumented immigrants earn at worst 5 percent less and at best the same amount as legal workers (Massey 1987; Rivera-Batiz 1999). These findings do not mean that discrimination does not take place, but simply that the majority of undocumented immigrants earn wages appropriate for their skills, productivity, and work experience. Although there is no evidence of systematic discrimination based on legal status, cases of discrimination are nevertheless disturbing. The law needs to be applied just as vigorously to individuals who mistreat immigrants as immigration laws are applied in deporting undocumented immigrants.

One reason why discrimination may not be uncovered in the majority of studies is because undocumented immigrants are rational economic beings who respond to unfair wages or conditions by "voting with their feet"; that is, they seek other employment. For example, if a particular employer cheats an undocumented worker, he or she is unlikely to accept this discrimination for a long period. The natural response for someone who is afraid to report abuse is to find another employer. When employees are free to choose their employer, employers who cheat or abuse their workers will lose them to employers who treat their workers fairly. Therefore, as long as undocumented immigrants are free and mobile within the black labor market, they should not encounter working conditions that are significantly different from those of other similar workers. The evidence suggests this is generally true, although Rothenberg (1998) provides examples to the contrary.

Naturalization

Naturalization is the process by which a foreign-born person becomes an American citizen. Naturalization is important for many reasons in the current political climate that favors restricting, and in some cases, eliminating legal immigrants' access to certain government programs. Only by becoming American citizens can immigrants have a voice in determining laws by voting, and as American citizens it is much more difficult to take away their rights. (However, there are several examples, such as the deportation of Mexican Americans during the 1930s, when American citizenship did not protect people from government-led discrimination.)

In order to become a naturalized American citizen, an immigrant must meet several requirements, the most significant of which are (1) having been a legal permanent resident of the United States for five years, (2) being fluent in English, (3) passing an examination on American history and civics, (4) submitting form N-400, along with an application fee of $225 per family, and (5) being of good moral character (INS 1997).

Although Canadian immigrants historically have had lower levels of naturalization than Mexicans, Mexican immigrants have long been singled out for their unwillingness to become American, as symbolized by American citizenship (DeSipio and de la Garza 1998). John Miller, a writer for the conservative magazine *The National Review* listed four principles of Americanization, the most important of which was becoming an American citizen: "The fourth [principle] is very important. You become an American by becoming a citizen and that means adhering to a set of political ideals that this country is founded on" (quoted in Hopkins 1999, 40). The implication is that immigrants who do not become citizens are rejecting American ideals.

Examining past Mexican naturalization rates might suggest that Mexican immigrants are hesitant to **acculturate** or assimilate. For example, by 1992, 17 percent of Mexican immigrants who legally arrived in 1977 had become citizens (DeSipio and de la Garza 1998). In contrast, the naturalization rates were higher for immigrants from Europe (28 percent), South America (39 percent), and Asia (56 percent). Yet other immigrant groups have rates lower than or similar to Mexicans: only 13 percent of Canadians, and 16 and 18 percent of Italian and British immigrants, respectively, had been naturalized by 1992.

Several factors contributed to the low naturalization rates among Mexican immigrants. Among them are the geographic proximity of Mexico, the legal status of undocumented immigrants that prevents them from becoming citizens even if they desire to, now-repealed Mexican laws that limited ownership of land by non-Mexican citizens, and insufficient years of legal residency.

Since 1992, however, significant changes have taken place that have altered the Mexican naturalization rate. Beginning after 1992 many Mexican immigrants legalized under IRCA beginning in 1987 became eligible for citizenship. As these immigrants had lived a life where they faced the continual vulnerability of not having legal protection, it is not surprising that they took the step of obtaining a higher level of protection by becoming citizens. The anti-immigration laws passed in the United States over the past fifteen years, including Proposition 187 in California and more recent federal legislation, have been another strong motivating factor. In 1997, for example, permanent residents became ineligible for various entitlement programs such as cash assistance and food stamps (INS 1997). Although Proposition 187 was found unconstitutional, the atmosphere in the United States against legal and undocumented immigrants alike has made Mexican immigrants more aware of the importance of protecting their rights by attaining citizenship. Moreover, in 1998, after several years of debate and partly in response to the harsh anti-immigration laws in the United States, the Mexican Congress passed laws permitting Mexicans abroad to hold dual citizenship (Danini 1998). Dual citizenship permits Mexicans to become American citizens without losing their Mexican nationality or prop-

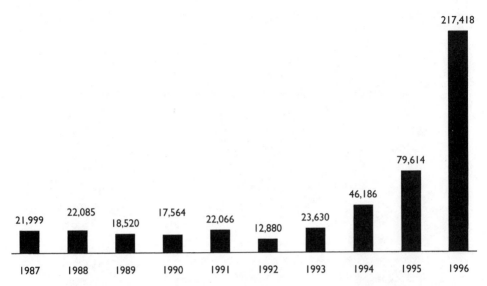

217,418

79,614

46,186

21,999   22,085   18,520   17,564   22,066   12,880   23,630

1987   1988   1989   1990   1991   1992   1993   1994   1995   1996

Figure 9. Number of naturalized Mexican immigrants, fiscal years 1987–1996. (Source: INS 1997)

erty ownership rights. For many immigrants, this means that they no longer have to choose between loyalty to their home or adopted country.

These circumstances have resulted in a huge increase in naturalization applications among Mexican immigrants. By 1995, 22 percent of Mexican immigrants who had entered in 1977 had become naturalized citizens (INS 1997), and by 1996, Mexico was the top country of birth for persons applying for naturalization. The roughly 255,000 immigrants submitting applications in 1996 represented a 200 percent increase in applications from 1995, and nearly half of these applicants were IRCA permanent residents. Cuba was a distant second country of birth with 63,000 applicants (INS 1997).

Figure 9 charts the growth in the number of naturalized Mexican immigrants from 1987 to 1996. Even after accounting for the fact that new legal Mexican immigrants are admitted each year, beginning around 1994 there is a clear increase in the number of immigrants who are becoming American citizens. From 1987 to 1993, the number of approved naturalization applications fluctuated around 20,000 per year. But in 1994, there was a 100 percent increase in the naturalization rate, followed by an increase of another 75 percent in 1995 and a 173 percent increase in 1996.

Topic Highlight: **The Significance of Naturalization**

Pacific Boulevard in Huntington Park has been known as the Main Street of Latino Los Angeles, but over the last decade it has become the center of another social transformation. Huntington Park is home to more new voters than any other area in Los Angeles County. Since 1994, voter registration has risen 36 percent, a rate seven times the countywide increase. Registered voters are still rare in these neighborhoods—perhaps a dozen on an entire block. However, their lives and aspirations provide insight into the growth of the Latino electorate that accompanies the growth in naturalization shown in figure 9.

One thing the new voters share in common is a growing recognition that becoming citizens and full-fledged participants in the American political process amplifies a voice that had been muted. New citizens treasure the right to vote. For many, the very act is seen as a statement of personal defiance, the exercising of a right that is all the more precious because of the social realities that still keep a large share of the community disenfranchised.

"I think it can change things if there are a lot of us voters," said Virginia Prieto, a worker at a local food-packing plant. "That's why I became a citizen." Like many new voters, Prieto, who moved to California from Mexico in 1974, sees casting her ballot as an achievement at the end of her family's long struggle to improve their lot and become U.S. citizens. "It was a sacrifice to become a citizen, because I'm always working and there's chores to do," Prieto said. "I studied all my lessons here at home. God helped me pass the test and answer all those questions."

César Salas, a first-generation Mexican American, is the first member of his family to vote in this country. He has not missed an election since turning eighteen and registering to vote in 1996, voting even in local elections where turnout is very low. He is also an avid reader of campaign literature. "A lot of people can't vote. I think it's like a gift," said Salas, an employee of a Pacific Boulevard movie theater. "If you can vote, vote." (From Tobar 1998) ■

Clearly, 1994 marked the beginning of a change in naturalization patterns for Mexican immigrants. As naturalized citizens have been shown to have higher levels of political participation than the average U.S.–born person, one likely result of this change is increased political participation and representation by Mexican Americans (Tobar 1998). The extent to which Mexican Americans will be able to translate citizenship into policy changes remains to be determined. It will, however, be interesting to tally voter turnout in upcoming elections.

■ Summary

Mexican immigrants comprise the single largest country-of-origin group in the United States, accounting for nearly 30 percent of all immigrants in March 1999. In general, Mexican immigrants are younger, poorer, have larger families, are more likely to work, and are more likely to use public assistance programs than U.S.–born persons.

The economic impact of Mexican legal and illegal immigration is a serious issue among those interested in limiting immigration. Most studies indicate, however, that the economic impact of immigration is at worst mildly negative and at best positive, so the underlying motivations for limiting immigration may be cultural fears about nonwhite immigrants.

The proximity of Mexico significantly influences the lives of Mexican immigrants, particularly in settlement and assimilation patterns. Mexican immigrants tend to live with other immigrants and are concentrated in the Southwest, particularly California and Texas. At the same time, however, relatively large numbers of Mexican immigrants also live in other states of the country, such as North Carolina and Washington, that are not traditionally associated with Mexican immigration. Many reside temporarily in the United States, doing seasonal labor. Measures of assimilation, such as wage parity and naturalization, indicate that Mexicans improve their economic situation over time, but in some instances they earn about 10 percent less than natives.

Naturalization rates among Mexican immigrants, traditionally among the lowest of all country-of-origin groups, have been increasing significantly. For the first time Mexicans are the largest national-origin group applying for naturalization, so it is possible that increasing political participation by these new citizens will temper anti-immigration sentiment in the United States.

■ Discussion Questions

1. What are the implications of the youthfulness of the immigrant population in terms of education and health?

2. Do you believe immigrants pose an economic threat at the local, state, or federal levels? Why or why not?

3. What conditions must be true for the displacement theory to be true?

4. What are some of the factors that account for the higher incidence of poverty among Mexican immigrants?

5. Where do Mexican immigrants tend to settle? Why do they settle in these areas?

6. What are the major requirements for becoming a U.S. citizen? Why are Mexicans now applying for naturalization at a higher rate than any other national-origin group?

■ Suggested Readings

Borjas, George J. 1982. The Labor Supply of Male Hispanic Immigrants in the United States. *International Migration Review* 17, 343–53.

——. 1991. *Friends or Strangers: The Impact of Immigrants on the U.S. Economy.* New York: Basic Books.

Delgado Bernal, Dolores. 1998. Chicana/o Education from the Civil Rights Era to the Present. In *The Elusive Quest for Equality: 150 Years of Chicana/Chicano Education,* edited by José F. Moreno. Cambridge, Mass.: Harvard Educational Review Publishing Group.

Rothenberg, Daniel. 1998. *With These Hands.* New York: Harcourt Brace.

Smith, James P., and Barry Edmonston, eds. 1997. *The New Americans: Economic, Demographic, and Fiscal Effects of Immigration.* Washington, D.C.: National Academy Press.

Vernez, Georges, Allan Abrahamse, and Denise Quigley. 1996. *How Immigrants Fare in U.S. Education.* Santa Monica, Calif.: Rand Corporation.

4

Going to School

THE EDUCATION OF MEXICAN AMERICANS

A **Chicana** civil rights lawyer comments, "Nobody told me what I needed to do to get into college. The counselors wanted me to go to junior college even though I graduated at the top of my class. But there was no expectation for Chicanas to be going to school. . . . I think because no other Chicanos had gone to college, they really didn't know what to do with us. . . . [My uncle] gave me an idea about what I needed to do, and I filled out the applications." (Gandara 1995, 103)

One area in which Mexican Americans differ substantially from the average American is in educational attainment. Low levels of education are a key reason why Mexican Americans have disproportionately higher poverty rates, lower incomes, and lower **socioeconomic status** than other Americans. Education is the best means for overcoming any obstacles that Mexican Americans may encounter as they search for *buenos días*. Increasing the educational level of Mexican Americans is perhaps the most important step in promoting economic **assimilation.**

This chapter examines the current educational status of Mexican Americans by generation to analyze how education affects their lives. First, it reviews the overall education level of Mexican Americans in order to compare their standing relative to other groups, in particular to non-Hispanic whites. Because economic mobility now requires more than a high-school education, it also details the postsecondary achievement of Mexican Americans.

In addition to analysis, this chapter provides some explanations and models of educational attainment by Mexican Americans. In keeping with the theme of the book, it is shown that successive generations of Mexican Americans have progressively higher levels of education. Even when educational achievement is narrowly defined as either years of school completed or degree completion, this measure shows that Mexican Americans are steadily climbing the educational ladder but have yet to attain educational parity with non-Hispanic whites.

■ Educational Profile

The education levels of Mexican Americans are an outcome of the interplay of various factors, including the education of their parents, the income and employment situation of the family, conditions at school, mentoring, discrimination and tracking into nonacademic tracks, peer and neighborhood effects, and individual ability and motivation. Petra, a mother of six, describes some of the struggles unique to Mexican Americans that limit their education:

> "I have two children that dropped out and I have three that graduated. I have six. The ones who graduated are doing well now. Two of them are married and have their own homes and they have good jobs and are doing fine. And the other one has a good job. And the two who dropped out, they are not bad kids, but they can't find jobs. . . ." Although Petra wanted [her son] James to get his high-school diploma, her own lack of an education made it impossible for her to help James with his schoolwork. She had dropped out of school in the sixth grade. She explained, "Well, if it was up to me I would have kept going because I love school. And I was good in school, but in those days they didn't force you to go. If you didn't go, they didn't say anything. They don't talk to your parents or see why you're not going. And my parents, they used to, well my father, he used to go to work in the fields to other towns and he used to pull us out of school and take us to work." (Romo and Falbo 1996, 26)

Putting these factors aside for later analysis, the chapter first examines the current education situation of Mexican Americans. Table 4 presents the average years of schooling of Mexican Americans, non–Mexican Americans including whites, and non-Hispanic whites specifically, who are used as the comparison group. Because different age groups and generations experience different circumstances that affect educational outcomes, the table is broken down into three generations and four age groups. In addition, because those over age twenty-five have more than likely completed their education whereas younger people may be in the process of completing their total education, table 4 includes only persons twenty-five years of age and older.

Table 4 Average Years of Education and Education Ratio, by Generation and Age

Age	FIRST Years	FIRST Ratio	SECOND Years	SECOND Ratio	THIRD Years	THIRD Ratio	TOTAL Years	TOTAL Ratio
MEXICAN AMERICAN								
Total	8.7	0.65	11.5	0.87	11.9	0.89	10.1	0.76
25–34	9.6	0.66	12.6	0.88	12.4	0.90	10.7	0.78
35–50	8.5	0.61	12.1	0.85	12.2	0.89	10.3	0.75
51–65	7.3	0.56	10.8	0.78	11.2	0.85	9.3	0.70
66+	6.1	0.54	9.0	0.74	9.1	0.75	7.9	0.65
NON–MEXICAN AMERICAN								
Total	12.9	0.98	13.2	1.01	13.2	0.99	13.2	0.99
25–34	13.8	0.95	14.3	1.00	13.6	0.99	13.6	0.99
35–50	13.3	0.95	14.3	0.99	13.6	0.99	13.6	0.99
51–65	12.6	0.96	13.9	1.00	13.1	0.99	13.1	0.99
66+	11.1	0.97	12.1	1.00	11.9	0.98	11.9	0.98
NON-HISPANIC WHITE								
Total	13.2	1.00	13.2	1.00	13.3	1.00	13.3	1.00
25–34	14.5	1.00	14.3	1.00	13.7	1.00	13.8	1.00
35–50	13.9	1.00	14.4	1.00	13.7	1.00	13.7	1.00
51–65	13.2	1.00	13.9	1.00	13.3	1.00	13.3	1.00
66+	11.4	1.00	12.1	1.00	12.1	1.00	12.1	1.00

Source: Author's weighted tabulations from the March 1999 Current Population Survey.
Notes: The highest-grade-completed education variable in the Current Population Survey is linearized as follows: less than first grade = 0 school years; first to fourth grades = 2.5 years; fifth or sixth grade = 5.5; seventh or eighth grades = 7.5; ninth grade = 9; tenth grade = 10; eleventh or twelfth grade without diploma = 11; high school diploma or GED = 12; some college = 13; associate's degree = 14; bachelor's degree = 16; master's degree = 18; professional degree or doctorate = 20. The education ratio is calculated relative to non-Hispanic whites in the same age group and generation. The sample includes persons age twenty-five and older, excluding those in group quarters.

The first characteristic of note in table 4 is that Mexicans of every generation have less education than the rest of the U.S. population. Overall, Mexican Americans average 10.1 years of education, whereas non–Mexican Americans average 13.2 years and non-Hispanic whites average 13.3 years of schooling. The educational deficit between Mexican Americans and European Americans is more than three school years. Another way to view this deficit is via an **education ratio**, or the number of years of schooling completed by Mexican Americans divided by the years of schooling completed by non-Hispanic whites in the same age group. Thus, the education ratio indicates whether Mexican Americans are catching up to or falling behind their European American counterparts. Ratios approaching 1.00 reflect equal levels of education between the two groups (or **educational assimilation**). As a group, Mexican Americans average 76 percent of the education of whites. Figure 10 plots the education ratios for first-, second-, and third-generation Mexican Americans given in table 4.

As this figure clearly shows, generation and age are important correlates with lower education for Mexican Americans. Generation alone explains some of the difference: each succeeding generation of Mexican Americans reduces the educational gap with non-Hispanic whites, in both real and relative terms. First-generation Mexican Americans have 65 percent of the education of European Americans, the second generation 87 percent, and the third generation 89 percent (see table 4). Mexican Americans never achieve parity with non-Hispanic whites in part because the latter are also increasing their levels of education. Still Mexican Americans are outpacing European Americans in educational gains from one generation to the next. It is worth noting, however, that Chapa (1988), who used pre-1980 data, reached the opposite conclusion.

The educational deficit of Mexican Americans is also highly sensitive to age. Within each generation of Mexican Americans, younger individuals have more education as well as a higher education ratio. In particular, the 25–34 age group of Mexican Americans has a higher average level of education than do older Mexican Americans. Within each generation, the 25–34 age group averages a half-year more schooling than older age groups, and second- and third-generation Mexican Americans in this group average more than twelve years of schooling. The overall average of 10.1 years of education for Mexican Americans is pulled down largely by the first generation (with 8.7 average years of education). Across generations, younger individuals have more education as well as a higher education ratio. For example, the average years of schooling and education ratio of second-generation Mexican Americans in the 35–50 age group is 12.1 and 0.85, respectively, whereas these figures are 12.4 and 0.90 for the third-generation 25–34 age group. Figure 10 illustrates how the educational improvement of Mexican Americans is evident across generations and age groups.

The small drop in education of the youngest group between the second and third generations (12.6 to 12.4) indicates at worst stagnation in educational achievement, and at best reflects the overall decline in education among *all* third-generation ethnic groups. Whereas other groups experience declines of a half-year or more, however, the decline among Mexican

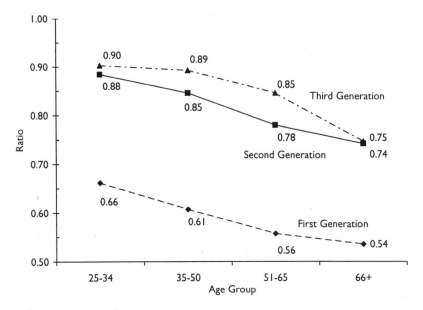

Figure 10. Education of Mexican Americans relative to non-Hispanic whites. Plotted from data in table 4. (Source: Author's weighted tabulations from the March 1999 Current Population Survey)

Americans is only two months, suggesting again that Mexican Americans are in the process of reducing the education gap with European Americans. The findings presented in this book contradict those of other studies, including Chapa (1988) and Zsembik and Llanes (1996), which found that Mexican Americans were not achieving educational assimilation. However, because these studies were based on older data and failed to separate data for different age groups, the findings are suspect.

■ Secondary Education

Contrary to the popular perception, the majority of U.S.–born Mexican Americans are high-school graduates. Table 5 estimates for Mexican Americans, non–Mexican Americans, and non-Hispanic whites the percentage of the population that has at least a high-school diploma. The simple average calculated over all Mexican Americans indicates that 52.9 percent has a high-school diploma or more, an education ratio of 0.60 compared to non-Hispanic whites. These are in truth very distressing statistics, but it is important to recognize that they result from combining Mexican Americans of different generations and age groups. The frequent

Table 5 Percentage of the Population with at Least a High-School Diploma

Age	FIRST		SECOND		THIRD		TOTAL	
	Percent	Ratio	Percent	Ratio	Percent	Ratio	Percent	Ratio
MEXICAN AMERICAN								
Total	36.6%	0.44	68.7%	0.82	74.1%	0.84	52.9%	0.60
25–34	41.0%	0.44	80.8%	0.85	79.1%	0.85	56.3%	0.60
35–50	35.9%	0.41	75.3%	0.78	79.5%	0.85	55.8%	0.60
51–65	26.2%	0.31	62.3%	0.68	62.7%	0.71	45.3%	0.51
66+	34.6%	0.52	42.0%	0.58	43.4%	0.60	39.2%	0.54
NON–MEXICAN AMERICAN								
Total	78.4%	0.95	84.5%	1.01	87.0%	0.98	86.0%	0.98
25–34	85.6%	0.93	94.9%	1.00	92.1%	0.99	91.5%	0.98
35–50	81.7%	0.93	95.4%	0.99	91.9%	0.99	91.0%	0.98
51–65	76.0%	0.90	91.6%	1.00	85.9%	0.98	85.3%	0.97
66+	62.4%	0.93	72.5%	1.01	69.7%	0.96	69.6%	0.96
NON-HISPANIC WHITE								
Total	82.5%	1.00	83.7%	1.00	88.5%	1.00	87.8%	1.00
25–34	92.4%	1.00	94.7%	1.00	93.2%	1.00	93.3%	1.00
35–50	87.8%	1.00	96.4%	1.00	93.0%	1.00	93.0%	1.00
51–65	84.2%	1.00	91.8%	1.00	87.9%	1.00	88.1%	1.00
66+	67.0%	1.00	72.0%	1.00	72.8%	1.00	72.3%	1.00

Source: Author's weighted tabulations from the March 1999 Current Population Survey.
Notes: Includes GED. Ratio is calculated relative to non-Hispanic whites in the same age group. Sample includes persons age twenty-five and older, excluding those living in group quarters.

reporting of aggregate statistics such as these portrays a very bleak picture of Mexican American high-school graduation rates. Rumberger (1991), for example, fails to distinguish the combined effects of age and generation in his analysis of dropout rates.

Even without considering the effects of age, the top panel shows a dramatic difference among first-, second-, and third-generation Mexican Americans. Among Mexican immigrants, only 36.6 percent have at least a high-school diploma, but two-thirds and three-quarters of the second and third generations, respectively, have at least graduated from high school. By the third generation the education ratio is 84 percent, showing continued growth with each succeeding generation of Mexican American students, not only in real terms, but also in relative terms. To illustrate this point more clearly, figure 11 plots as a graph the data given in table 5.

Although each younger Mexican American cohort of every generation

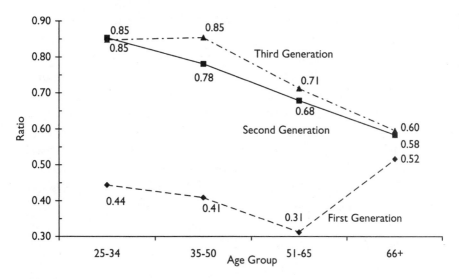

Figure 11. High-school graduation ratios for Mexican Americans relative to non-Hispanic whites. Plotted from data in table 5. (Source: Author's weighted tabulations from the March 1999 Current Population Survey)

improves its education, a delineation can be made between those who are younger versus older than fifty. It is not surprising that younger Mexican Americans within each generation have higher levels of education than their older counterparts. Secular public education has become increasingly more available over the twentieth century, so that regardless of ethnic group, students born in the late twentieth century have completed more years of schooling than those born earlier in the century. Another factor is the improved educational opportunities for Mexican Americans resulting from reduction in discrimination at school. For example, it was legal to segregate Mexican American students from white students up until the late 1940s (Delgado Bernal 1998; Monroy 1999). Other discriminatory practices have included tracking Mexican American students into vocational courses, shoddy school capital, and a general lack of interest by educators in improving the education of Mexican Americans (Carter and Segura 1979; Gandara 1995; Hernández 1973; Solórzano and Solórzano 1995).

In addition, Mexican Americans are the only ethnic group for which the percentage of persons with at least a high-school diploma increases from one generation to the next in every age group. The percentage of high-school graduates is around 80 percent among third-generation Mexican

Americans younger than fifty-one years of age. Perhaps more significantly, their education ratio is greater than that of their second-generation peers.

In contrast, the education of older third-generation Mexican Americans is significantly lower than for both younger Mexican Americans and European Americans. Second- and third-generation Mexican Americans ages fifty-one to sixty-five have 68 and 71 percent of the education of similar whites. An interesting feature of the data is that the education ratio of first-generation Mexican immigrants over age sixty-five is 52 percent, a ratio higher than those for *all* younger Mexican immigrants. One can infer that many of these early-twentieth-century immigrants were political refugees from **Porfirio Díaz's** political oppression and as such may have been more educated than subsequent economic immigrants. These early immigrants are not representative of the current Mexican immigrant population.

College Education

Prior to the 1980s, a high-school degree was often sufficient to get a well-paying job. However, structural changes in the U.S. economy since then have increased the educational requirements for well-paying and high-status jobs (Santos and Seitz 1992). A postsecondary education is therefore a prerequisite for the present and future economic mobility of Mexican Americans. In addition, for Mexican Americans to keep pace with increases in education among non-Hispanic whites, they need to attend and graduate from college in greater numbers.

Table 6 examines the postsecondary educational attainment of Mexican Americans, non–Mexican Americans, and non-Hispanic whites who have at least some college experience. In general, within each generation and age group, Mexican Americans are more likely to attend college without attaining a degree than any other population of Americans. For example, 58.1 percent of first-generation Mexican Americans between the ages of twenty-five and thirty-four who attended college did not earn any type of degree. In contrast only 17.3 percent of similar non-Hispanic whites failed to attain some type of college degree.

Possible explanations for the higher dropout rate among minorities, especially Mexican Americans, include higher direct costs associated with college (tuition, books, room and board, taking tests, etc.), indirect costs of college attendance (foregone work income), and an unreceptive or outright hostile environment on campus. Since the high-school graduation rate

Table 6 Degree Attainment of College Attendees, by Generation

	FIRST			SECOND			THIRD		
Age	Dropout	AA/AS	BA/BS+	Dropout	AA/AS	BA/BS+	Dropout	AA/AS	BA/BS+
MEXICAN AMERICAN									
Total	52.0%	14.2%	33.8%	50.9%	20.7%	28.4%	55.1%	16.3%	28.6%
25–34	58.1%	13.3%	28.6%	50.9%	21.4%	27.7%	55.7%	18.7%	25.5%
35–50	44.4%	16.7%	39.0%	46.7%	20.9%	32.4%	55.9%	16.7%	27.5%
51–65	52.2%	8.2%	39.6%	57.8%	19.0%	23.2%	46.1%	10.9%	43.0%
66+	52.3%	15.7%	32.0%	57.5%	19.2%	23.4%	79.3%	6.6%	14.2%
NON–MEXICAN AMERICAN									
Total	24.7%	11.4%	63.9%	32.3%	13.7%	54.1%	35.3%	15.5%	49.2%
25–34	24.5%	10.6%	64.9%	27.0%	15.7%	57.2%	35.0%	15.8%	49.2%
35–50	24.3%	12.6%	63.1%	30.6%	13.4%	55.9%	32.9%	17.1%	50.0%
51–65	22.5%	10.0%	67.5%	31.3%	12.8%	56.0%	36.6%	13.4%	50.0%
66+	31.3%	11.9%	56.7%	38.6%	13.1%	48.3%	42.7%	12.5%	44.8%
NON-HISPANIC WHITE									
Total	22.9%	12.3%	64.9%	32.3%	13.4%	54.3%	33.6%	15.4%	51.0%
25–34	17.3%	12.2%	70.5%	26.1%	15.1%	58.9%	31.8%	15.6%	52.6%
35–50	20.3%	12.9%	66.8%	29.9%	13.2%	56.9%	31.2%	17.2%	51.6%
51–65	22.9%	11.7%	65.4%	31.2%	12.5%	56.3%	35.9%	13.2%	50.9%
65+	36.9%	11.6%	51.5%	38.8%	13.2%	48.0%	42.3%	12.3%	45.3%

Source: Author's weighted tabulations from the March 1999 Current Population Survey.
Notes: Sample includes persons age twenty-five and older, excluding those living in group quarters.

among older Mexican Americans has been low, it is likely that many Mexican American college attendees are the first in their family to do so. As a consequence, it is also possible that a lack of family members or peers who previously attended college and can provide mentorship and encouragement puts Mexican Americans at a disadvantage. The lack of advice, financial aid, and a feeling of alienation on campus may prompt Mexican American students to drop out at higher rates than other groups.

The only education level at which Mexican Americans outperform non-Hispanic whites is at the community college level. An average of about 20 percent of the two youngest age groups of second- and third-generation Mexican Americans have an associate's degree, compared to about 15 percent of whites.

In the aggregate, there is no great difference across generations or age groups in the bachelor's-degree completion rate for Mexican Americans. More than one-third of all Mexican Americans who attended college attained a bachelor's or graduate degree. One interesting pattern is the larger

Topic Highlight: An Example of Educational Achievement

Victoria DeFrancesco graduated with a bachelor's degree in political science. She is one of the 4 to 5 percent of Mexican American women who have at least a bachelor's degree. But she does not want to stop her education there—she has enrolled in a political science graduate program with the goal of getting a Ph.D. Her story exemplifies many of the factors that affect educational attainment in the Mexican American community.

DeFrancesco's parents are similar to many other Mexican American parents: they desire that their children get as much education as possible to better their opportunities. Many Mexican American parents, however, can offer only emotional support due to their low socioeconomic status. In DeFrancesco's case, her mother is from an upper-middle-class family in Sonora, Mexico, and her father is a lawyer who grew up in a working-class family. Although DeFrancesco's mother did not attend college because her father did not think it proper for women to get an education, she always valued a college education. Thus, between her mother's desire for an education and her father's actual college experience, DeFrancesco grew up in a family where a college education was important. On the other hand, DeFrancesco's family did not pressure her in any particular direction.

Another important factor in DeFrancesco's academic success story is the presence of positive role models inside and outside the family. Positive role models serve not only as motivators, but also as proof that hard work and ambition pay dividends. She points not only to the examples her parents set, but also to the achievements of her older sister, now a veterinarian. Furthermore, her high-school teachers and college professors all encouraged her academic ambitions. Female role models—her mother, her sister, and female college professors—have been of particular importance because the educational expectations for Hispanic women may be lower and the value of their education sometimes questioned. Finally, DeFrancesco's ambition and determination should not be underestimated. She is an example of what Mexican Americans can accomplish when individual effort is reinforced by equal opportunities and not hindered by socioeconomic factors. ■

percentage of first-generation college attendees who attain at least a bachelor's degree. This pattern holds among all three ethnic groups examined in table 6. One explanation is that those Mexican American students in the first generation who are able to attend college are a select few and share similar backgrounds, such as being among the first in their families to attend college.

Separating ethnic groups by age and generation does not explain the lower college achievement of Mexican Americans. Given that high-school graduation rates are improving, the next challenge for Mexican Americans and for U.S. educational policy is to improve the retention and graduation of Mexican American college students.

▉ Economic Incentives to Invest in Education

Although table 4 shows that Mexican Americans have made clear progress, they continue to have less education than non-Hispanic whites (and in fact all other major ethnic groups). Why do Mexican Americans have fewer average years of education? Various explanations exist, but it is worthwhile to begin with an economic perspective on educational attainment.

An individual's education level is thought to be the outcome of a rational decision in which that person examines the various alternatives at various stages in life, and then chooses the option best suited for him or her. In particular, the two most common options for individuals in their late teens are school or work. Potential students choose between postsecondary schooling or work based upon the future financial rewards offered by each option. Students who believe an additional semester or year of schooling will increase lifetime earnings by more than the amount of income they could earn by working during the same period will continue their education. Students continue to attain more schooling until no further monetary gains can be made relative to the foregone work income. Although nonfinancial benefits of education also play a role in the decision to continue one's education, the financial rewards of education are the primary motive for furthering education beyond the time required by mandatory attendance laws (usually age sixteen). The bottom line is that individuals continue to attain education as long as the income they forego by going to school is less than the increase in future income resulting from this additional education.

Figure 12 illustrates this principle. Take, for example, a student

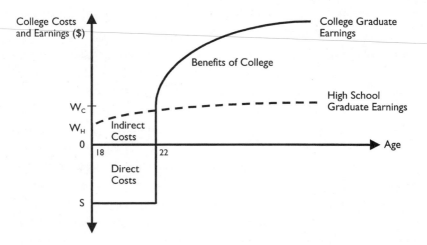

■ Figure 12. The decision to work or attend college.

contemplating whether to stop his or her education after high school or to continue on and attain a bachelor's degree. If the individual starts working immediately after high school, he or she will begin earning income, whereas completing a bachelor's degree involves the direct cost of school as well as the indirect cost of the income foregone during the college years. Direct costs—including tuition, room and board, and other education-related expenses—can exceed $30,000 per year at some private colleges. The indirect costs include not only the income lost while being a full-time student for four years, but the psychological costs of attending college, such as being subjected to examinations or long and tedious courses (Ehrenberg and Smith 1994).

A high-school graduate who begins to work immediately will commence earning a wage of W_H and experience gradual increases in earnings for the rest of his or her working life. On the other hand, a person who chooses to attend college pays S in direct costs for four years. The total cost of attending college, however, includes not only S but also the indirect costs of attending college, represented by the area below the earnings profile of high-school graduates and above the horizontal axis. This college graduate begins work at the age of twenty-two and earns a wage of W_C, which may or may not be higher than W_H, depending on various factors. Due to the postsecondary education, however, the college graduate experiences faster growth in wages and thus, over his or her lifetime, earns more than the high-school graduate. As figure 12 is drawn, the area encompassed by the direct and indirect costs is smaller than the area represented by the earnings benefits of a college degree, so one would predict that a person in this situation would choose to go to college based on monetary reasons. On the other hand, if the earnings profile for a high-school graduate were steeper, and the direct and indirect costs of a college education were higher than shown, at some point the monetary advantage would evaporate and the optimal choice would be not to get a bachelor's degree.

Since the 1980s, the wage gap between college and high-school graduates has widened, suggesting that significant financial incentives to get a bachelor's degree presently exist. Whereas in 1975 college graduates earned 50 percent more than high-school graduates for **full-time,** year-round work, by 1990 the difference had increased to 64 percent (Ehrenberg and Smith 1994). This rising income inequality resulted from a slight growth in earnings for those with a bachelor's degree coupled with falling earnings for high-school graduates. Given the incentives to attend and graduate from college, why do larger numbers of Mexican Americans not graduate from college?

One possible answer is that even if Mexican Americans complete college, they will not reap the same economic rewards as non-Hispanic whites due to discrimination. If the returns (monetary value) of education are indeed lower for Mexican Americans, then they have a lesser economic incentive to attain education than non-Hispanic whites do. The evidence, however, shows that systematic wage discrimination does not exist for well-educated Mexican Americans, although it may exist for jobs that require very little education (a laborer, for example; see chapter 6).

■ Factors Affecting the Investment in Education

Educational attainment is affected by many factors, including socioeconomic background, ability, school environment and conditions, encouragement from teachers and parents, occupational and educational goals, and motivation. Because Mexican Americans tend to be poorer than non-Hispanic whites, their socioeconomic status puts many at a disadvantage in the classroom. Socioeconomic status is an important factor in education because **middle-class** and upper-class families can provide a quiet area to study, computers, books and magazines, and other costly education-related materials. Moreover, wealthier families are more likely to live near good schools and in neighborhoods that promote learning and educational achievement. In addition, wealthier families tend to promote educational achievement and are able to support their children's educational aspirations.

Unfortunately, the reality is that students from low-income families are more likely to encounter difficulty financing a college education. Financial-aid packages to low-income students are usually insufficient to cover all of the expenses of a college education, and as a consequence high-ability students from low-income families are less likely to attend four-year colleges. For example, 44 percent of high-ability students from low-income families versus 74 percent of similar students from high-income families enrolled in college (Ehrenberg and Smith 1994).

Socioeconomic status is also highly related to the level of education of the parents. Well-educated parents not only serve as role models for their children, but also establish higher educational expectations. In addition, these parents are more capable of helping their children with homework, answering questions about college, and offering firsthand experience and advice about school. For first- and second-generation Mexican American children, however, the impact of parental education may not be as significant as for other populations because the positive immigrant experience may outweigh the low education levels of immigrant parents (Santos and Seitz 1992).

Differences in ability (which encompasses intelligence, problem-solving skills, and other innate abilities) is not a valid explanation for the lower educational levels of Mexican Americans (Carter and Segura 1979; Delgado Bernal 1998). Because Asians and whites, on average, score higher on IQ tests, some have argued incorrectly that Mexican Americans are genetically less intelligent than other races (Solórzano and Solórzano 1995). In the education system, this conclusion has justified and continues to justify the tracking of Mexican American students into nonacademic courses and results in generally lower academic expectations (Monroy 1999). The Chicana civil rights lawyer introduced in the beginning of the chapter is an example of someone with ability who suffered as a consequence of this practice.

Mexican American culture has also been characterized as being incompatible with academic success because it emphasizes present gratification over future payoffs, family interdependence over individual success, maintenance of Spanish at the expense of English proficiency, and a determinist attitude toward mobility and life in general (that is, that there is little people can do to influence what happens to them in life) (Carter and Segura 1979; Delgado Bernal 1998; Solis 1995; Solórzano and Solórzano 1995; Suárez-Orozco and Suárez-Orozco 1995). For those who believe this **cultural deficit model**, the prescription in the classroom has been to "fix" the cultural characteristics that Mexican American students acquire at home by eliminating all traces of their culture. Several studies, including Carter and Segura (1979), refute the cultural deficit model, however. Furthermore, Suárez-Orozco and Suárez-Orozco (1995) find that Mexican American culture stresses self-initiated achievement and the hard work necessary for achievement, while at the same time emphasizing familial ties and cooperation. Thus the culture of Mexican American students is not inconsistent with academic success.

Although school quality has not conclusively been found to affect cognitive development, there is evidence that schools with a commitment to strong bilingual, cultural, and academic programs that value the students' culture offer Mexican Americans more motivation to continue their education (Zsembik and Llanes 1996). This statement should not be misinterpreted as suggesting that mainstream American culture is itself deficient, or that Mexican American students can learn only when the curriculum is centered around Mexican American culture. Rather, it means that the educators should not treat Mexican American students as requiring remedial education, but instead should challenge them academically and encourage them to further their education to the greatest possible extent.

The importance of neighborhood and peer effects should not be minimized. Both positive and negative role models influence students' outlook regarding their future. If children are surrounded by role models of adults who have gone to college and attained a meaningful level of success, they will recognize the economic rewards of a college education. If, on the other hand, children continually see role models who, despite their best efforts, have not succeeded, then the economic rewards of education may seem out of reach for them as well. Indeed, students living in neighborhoods with well-educated persons do better than those who live in neighborhoods where people have less education (Borjas 1995).

Generational status and English- and Spanish-language ability are two unique characteristics of Mexican Americans that also potentially affect educational performance. Due to both the Mexican legacy in the Southwest and the arrival of a record number of immigrants, Spanish-language use is a significant fact of life among many Mexican American children. Prior to the 1970s, teachers and community leaders generally frowned upon the use of Spanish at schools, and students who did not speak and understand English received a substandard education (Delgado Bernal 1998). Bilingual education, established nationally through federal legislation in 1968, was intended to bridge the language barrier by teaching subject material in students' native language while at the same time teaching them English. Over time, instruction in English would dominate as students mastered the language. Recently, bilingual education has become a heated political issue. An alternative approach is an English as a second language (ESL) program, which is a structured program similar to foreign language instruction, generally conducted mostly or entirely in English (Ovando and Collier 1998).

Generational status influences educational attainment because Mexican Americans, like previous immigrant groups such as Irish, Russians, and Italians, tend to be at the bottom of the socioeconomic ladder. Many believe that over time Mexican Americans will assimilate to American cultural norms and slowly improve their status, including educational levels. Proponents of this theory (see, for example, Chávez 1991) argue that the large number of first- and second-generation Mexican Americans makes it difficult to fully appreciate and ascertain their movement "out of the barrio" and into the American mainstream. This classical assimilation hypothesis predicts that educational achievement will increase with number of generations in the United States. In fact, the evidence presented previously supports this hypothesis.

Alternatively, the **immigrant optimism** theory argues that Mexican immigrant children and American-born children of Mexican immigrants may actually perform better than expected because they have greater than average ambition and drive (Kao and Tienda 1995). Much of a child's ambition to do well in school results from the emphasis that his or her parents put on education as a means to secure a better place in the economy and society. Students with an immigrant background tend to be poorer, grow up not speaking English, have less-educated parents, and attend overcrowded and understaffed schools that do not always meet their needs. Yet many overcome these hurdles to perform better than assimilationist models would predict. Since a large percentage of Mexican Americans are first- or second-generation students, this theory potentially has significant implications for their educational achievement.

On the other hand, long-term socioeconomic stagnation among U.S.–

born Mexican Americans may create antisocial and rebellious attitudes toward educational achievement (this theory is analogous to the **underclass** model of persistent poverty; see chapter 5). Mexican Americans historically have been marginalized and denied equal opportunities in U.S. society, especially with regard to education (Monroy 1999). As a consequence of this negative environment, U.S.–born, "assimilated" Mexican Americans may disengage from and devalue schooling (Schmader, Major, and Gramzow 1998). The **cholo** subculture is an example of a Mexican American group that identifies with neither Mexican nor American notions of success. Many cholos grow up experiencing discrimination either first or second hand, and rather than identifying with positive role models, they rebel and believe that education will not improve their situation.

In general, several researchers—including Fligstein and Fernández (1985), González and de la Torre (2000), Mora (1997), and Zsembik and Llanes (1996)—have found that family background, especially the mother's education and socioeconomic status, affects the educational attainment of Mexican Americans. English language fluency is another factor that improves educational performance, while generational status has a gradual positive effect after the first generation.

◼ Summary

Mexican Americans have not achieved the same success as non-Hispanic whites in terms of high-school and college completion. The indications are, however, that they are attaining more education and at a faster pace than are non-Hispanic whites or the rest of the U.S. population. The majority of European Americans have been living in the United States for more than three generations, whereas the majority of Mexican Americans are the direct offspring of first- or second-generation Mexican Americans. Therefore, the process of educational assimilation may not be complete for them.

The information presented in this chapter contradicts other studies which conclude that "a substantial portion of third generation Mexican Americans have educational levels that have shown no indication of converging with Anglo levels" (Chapa 1988, 6). In fact, the most recent data suggest the opposite—Mexican Americans are increasing their average educational levels at a faster rate than whites. The trend toward educational assimilation is clearly evident in the Mexican American community.

The question remains how best to increase and improve the education of

Mexican Americans. The lower educational levels for Mexican Americans shown in tables 4 to 6 are largely due to socioeconomic factors. If socioeconomic differences are not addressed, then it is unclear how improvements in the education of Mexican Americans can be achieved. In the end, what matters is whether the educational situation of Mexican Americans is improving given their current conditions. The evidence presented indicates that this is indeed taking place, but that future growth depends on college completion beyond the community college level. In order for Mexican Americans to continue increasing their education levels, economic theory states that the benefit must outweigh the cost. Schools must do a better job of ensuring that Mexican American students are exposed to the possibilities and rewards of a college education. In addition, schools must do a better job of overcoming the obstacles to educational achievement that socioeconomic status creates for Mexican American students. Lastly, Mexican American students must be exposed to positive role models who reinforce the importance of education, independent of the economic benefits.

■ Discussion Questions

1. What is the educational deficit between Mexican Americans and non-Hispanic whites? Does this gap differ with generational status?

2. How are the factors limiting the educational attainment of Mexican Americans different from those affecting other ethnic groups?

3. Why do younger Mexican Americans have higher levels of education than older Mexican Americans of the same generation?

4. Discuss the trends in Mexican American education at the college level.

5. What are the direct and indirect costs that students consider when contemplating whether to go to college?

6. Why do fewer Mexican Americans graduate from college compared to the U.S. population as a whole?

7. Are Mexican Americans inherently less capable of attaining an education than the rest of the U.S. population is?

▪ Suggested Readings

Delgado Bernal, Dolores. 1998. Chicana/o Education from the Civil Rights Era to the Present. In *The Elusive Quest for Equality: 150 Years of Chicana/Chicano Education,* edited by José F. Moreno. Cambridge, Mass.: Harvard Educational Review Publishing Group.

Gandara, Patricia. 1995. *Over the Ivy Wall: The Educational Mobility of Low-Income Chicanos.* Albany: State University of New York Press.

Kao, Grace, and Marta Tienda. 1995. Optimism and Achievement: The Educational Performance of Immigrant Youth. *Social Science Quarterly* 76, 1–19.

Monroy, Douglas. 1999. *Rebirth: Mexican Los Angeles from the Great Migration and the Great Depression.* Berkeley: University of California Press.

Ovando, Carlos J., and Virginia P. Collier. 1998. *Bilingual Education and ESL Classrooms: Teaching in Multicultural Contexts.* Boston, Mass: McGraw-Hill.

Romo, Harriet, and Toni Falbo. 1996. *Latino High School Graduation: Defying the Odds.* Austin: University of Texas Press.

Subiendo

TOWARD THE MIDDLE CLASS

When your parents come here [from Mexico], you see the struggles, the difficulties, the barriers with language, and it takes you a long time to get out of that stage. . . . For me, I knew that I had to [buy] a home as soon as I could because that's the only way out, that's the only way to have something for the future. (Theresa Arreguin, quoted in O'Neill 1994)

Mexican Americans suffer higher levels of poverty than most other ethnic groups. Whereas the poverty rate of Mexican American families has hovered just below 30 percent for most of the 1990s, the average poverty rate in the United States is 10 percent. This means that the Mexican population is almost three times more likely to live in poverty than the average American. To some social scientists, this statistic positions Mexican Americans as an **underclass** with limited prospects for economic mobility. The Mexican American population is traditionally portrayed as being poor, as enrolling in government transfer programs, and as having few prospects for economic mobility. Even though many noneconomic explanations for Mexican American poverty exist—for example, the continual influx of poor immigrants from Mexico—this perception is rarely challenged.

Income levels, poverty rates, and asset accumulation (the process of acquiring property with market value) are all indicators of the present economic status and future economic mobility of families and individuals. Therefore, in this chapter I explore the income distribution, extent of poverty, and measures of wealth and asset accumulation in the Mexican American population across generations, then compare these trends with those of other ethnic groups. That a large number of Mexican Americans have low levels of current and permanent income is undeniable. However, Mexican Americans are not in danger of becoming a permanent underclass, but rather are in the process of joining the ranks of the **middle class**. The findings indicate a slow progression in terms of higher income, lower poverty rates, and less reliance on public assistance programs, with smaller improvement in asset accumulation. Nevertheless, the evidence suggests that Mexican Americans are not an underclass. The **immigrant optimism** of first- and second-generation Mexican Americans, with its emphasis on hard work and education, enables the movement into the middle class.

■ Income Distribution

The stereotype that Mexican Americans are poor is repeated so many times in the popular media and generally accepted by the public that it has become a fixed image. The mixing of family-income data for Mexican immigrants and U.S.–born Mexican Americans results in a fuzzy and distorted picture of the Mexican American population. The circumstances of a third-generation Mexican American family are very different from those of a recent immigrant family, a fact obscured by many aggregate statistics.

Family income is derived from various sources, primarily, of course, wages, but also **dividends** from **assets**, inheritance, public assistance and welfare programs, gifts, and other sources.

Differences in family income are partly an outcome of immigration status, age of the head of household, English proficiency, region of residence, and most importantly, education. In general, it could be argued that generational status captures some of these differences. For this reason, figure 13 breaks down the total income levels of Mexican-origin families by generation based on 1998 statistics. For comparison, the vertical lines mark the 1998 poverty threshold for a family of four, the median income of all Mexican American families, and the median income of all non-Mexican-origin U.S. families. (The median is the point where half the population's incomes fall above, and half below, that value.)

Figure 13 shows that, when all generations are considered together, the median income for Mexican Americans is 57 percent of that of the rest of the U.S. population. Since the median divides the population in half, this means that the majority of Mexican American families are concentrated in the lower end of the range. Although smaller percentages of second- and third-generation families have incomes below the poverty line, no generation matches the median income of the rest of the U.S. population.

In all, about 37 percent of first-generation families earn less than $20,000, compared to about 29 percent of second- and third-generation families.

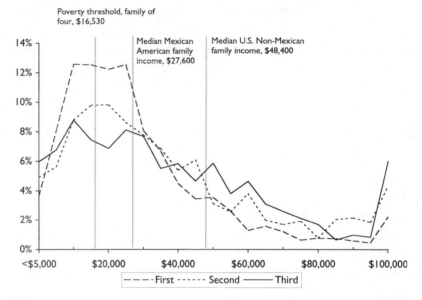

Poverty threshold, family of four, $16,530

Median Mexican American family income, $27,600

Median U.S. Non-Mexican family income, $48,400

First ----- Second ——— Third

■ Figure 13. Total 1998 income for Mexican American families by generation (as percentages of the population). Only primary families are counted. (Source: Author's weighted estimates from the March 1999 Current Population Survey)

Second-generation families have the lowest percentage of families with incomes below the poverty line. At the upper end of the income distribution, nearly 120,000 second- and third-generation families (about 5 percent), earned more than $100,000 in 1998, compared to only 52,000 (2 percent) of first-generation Mexican American families. Statistically speaking, third-generation families have a more equal distribution of income than do first- or second-generation families.

An unexpected and troubling finding is that there are more extremely poor third-generation than second-generation Mexican American families. Although the number of third-generation families exceeds the number of second-generation families by about 800,000, the percentage of families with less than $10,000 in total income is about 13 percent (or about 124,000) for the third generation, compared with 10 percent (or 45,000) for the second generation. It should be noted, however, that the same pattern is observed for non–Mexican American families: 9 percent of third-generation non–Mexican American families are in poverty, compared to 4 percent of the second generation.

At the same time, compared to the third generation, a greater percentage of second-generation families have incomes in the $10,000 to $35,000

Table 7 Mean and Median Family Income, Family Size, and Per Capita Income, by Generation

	FIRST		SECOND		THIRD		TOTAL	
	Mean	Median	Mean	Median	Mean	Median	Mean	Median
FAMILY INCOME								
Mexican American								
	$32,358	$25,000	$41,270	$30,800	$43,346	$34,000	$37,277	$27,600
Non–Mexican American								
	$60,738	$44,800	$67,357	$49,571	$60,828	$48,800	$61,274	$48,400
FAMILY SIZE								
Mexican American								
	4.2	4.0	3.4	3.0	3.6	3.0	3.9	4.0
Non–Mexican American								
	3.4	3.0	2.7	2.0	3.0	3.0	3.1	3.0
PER CAPITA FAMILY INCOME								
Mexican American								
	$ 8,523	$ 6,167	$13,392	$ 9,882	$13,379	$10,267	$10,862	$ 7,667
Non–Mexican American								
	$19,950	$13,517	$26,176	$18,479	$21,929	$16,551	$22,042	$16,410

Source: Author's weighted tabulations from the March 1999 Current Population Survey.
Note: Only primary families are counted.

range, but third-generation families are generally more likely to have incomes greater than $40,000. In summary, third-generation families are more diverse than earlier generations—there is a significant percentage of high-income families, just as there is a significant percentage of low-income families.

Table 7 shows the median and mean (average) incomes of Mexican American and non–Mexican American families (the same data used for figure 13), along with the median and average family sizes of both groups. The per capita income section divides income by family size to derive the amount available per family member. This table shows that the median family income of first-generation families is $25,000 compared to $30,800 and $34,000 for second- and third-generation families, respectively. In addition to having lower family incomes, first-generation families also have larger families, resulting in substantially less per capita income. Examining the first-generation column reveals that Mexican immigrant families have mean and median incomes that are a little more than half those of other immigrant families. Although second- and third-generation families remain worse off than their non-Mexican-origin counterparts, their per capita income is higher than that of first-generation families, indicating an improvement in overall standard of living.

Although Mexican American families are poorer than other families, their average and median incomes do increase from one generation to the next. In fact, Mexican Americans are unique in this respect: non–Mexican American families in the third generation have lower mean and median incomes than second-generation families do. For example, second-generation families in the United States average $67,400, but third-generation families average only $60,800, compared to mean incomes of $41,270 and $43,300, respectively, for Mexican Americans.

The questions that remain now are (1) Why do Mexican Americans have less income than their non–Mexican American counterparts? and (2) Will the incomes of future generations of Mexican Americans catch up to or surpass those of the typical American family?

Poverty

The data provide undeniable evidence of systematically low levels of income among the Mexican American population. This is especially true for first- and third-generation families. The poverty threshold in figure 13 and the income information in table 7 indicate that a large percentage of Mexican American families would be classified as poor by the federal government.

The federal definition of **poverty status** is an absolute measure based on a combination of family size, family characteristics, and income. Family characteristics considered in the definition of a poverty threshold include whether or not the family lives on a farm, family type (couple-, male-, or female-headed household), and the number of children in the family (U.S. Bureau of the Census 1999). Current poverty thresholds are adjusted for inflation but not for increased standard of living, which results in a growing difference between the poor and the rest of society as the overall standard of living in the United States improves (Schiller 1989). The federal poverty level is merely a convenient cutoff point established by the government to determine eligibility for various government assistance programs. It should not be taken as an absolute indicator of how much income is "enough" for subsistence living versus how much is not. There are many families above the poverty line whose standard of living the majority of the population would consider poor.

It is easy to count the number of people living in poverty once a definition is established, but it is more difficult to describe adequately the short-term and lasting effects of poverty. The effects of poverty range from not eating a full or nutritious meal, to lacking heating during the cold winter months, to having insufficient clothing and other amenities the majority of us take for granted. Given the large number of families and individuals of Mexican descent living at or below the poverty line, concern exists about the permanence of their situation. These concerns have resulted in programs that address the causes and symptoms of poverty through helping families find better jobs, ensuring access to education, keeping families intact, insuring access to antipoverty programs, and reducing the alleged abuse of public assistance and welfare programs by unentitled persons.

In the Family Poverty Rate and Person Poverty Rate sections of table 8, the first row shows the number of families or persons who were so categorized in 1998, and the second row gives the percentage of each generation that is in poverty. Based on the official definition of poverty, more than one-quarter of all Mexican American persons and more than one-fifth of families live in poverty. In contrast, the poverty rate for non–Mexican American individuals and families ranges from only 4 to 14 percent. This means that the incidence of poverty is about two and one-half times greater among Mexican-origin families and persons.

Of the total number of families and individuals classified as poor in 1998, about 16 percent were of Mexican descent. As Mexican American families represent only 6 percent of all U.S. families, it is clear that they are over-represented among the poor. Forty-five percent of all immigrant families in poverty in the United States are Mexican.

To examine the hypothesis that generational status plays a major role in poverty figures, it is worthwhile to note that poor first-generation families comprise 15 percent, while second- and third-generation families comprise only 3 and 6 percent, of all Mexican American families. First-generation families account for only 52 percent of all Mexican American families but 60 percent of all Mexican American families in poverty.

The percentage of each generation in poverty is an indication of the permanence of poverty; that is, decreasing percentages across generations would indicate movement out of poverty. First-generation Mexican Americans are more likely to be living in poverty than the second or third generation: 28 percent compared to 19 and 21 percent, respectively. This finding

Table 8 Unadjusted and Adjusted Poverty Rates, by Generation

	MEXICAN AMERICAN			NON–MEXICAN AMERICAN		
	First	Second	Third	First	Second	Third
FAMILY POVERTY						
Number	656,476	155,252	290,438	806,779	196,111	4,823,824
Percent	28.1%	19.4%	21.2%	13.3%	4.3%	8.7%
PERSON POVERTY						
Number	2,059,592	1,879,244	1,557,006	2,710,539	2,290,295	23,012,533
Percent	28.5%	29.1%	23.9%	14.1%	11.1%	11.1%
FAMILY POVERTY RATE ADJUSTED FOR:[1]						
Education	19.0%	15.2%	18.4%	13.3%	5.1%	9.4%
Education and age						
	14.9%	14.3%	16.8%	13.3%	9.1%	10.2%
Education, age, and family size and type						
	16.5%	13.4%	15.5%	13.3%	9.6%	10.5%
PERSON POVERTY RATE ADJUSTED FOR:[2]						
Education	21.2%	23.6%	20.1%	14.1%	9.6%	10.4%
Education and age						
	20.5%	22.5%	19.0%	14.1%	10.0%	10.4%
Education age, and family size and type						
	21.4%	23.1%	17.7%	14.1%	9.8%	10.2%

Source: Author's weighted tabulations from the March 1999 Current Population Survey.
Note: Excludes persons age fifteen and younger who are unrelated to the family.
[1]Estimated from a linear probability regression of poverty on characteristics, where poverty equals 1 if the family is in poverty and 0 otherwise. First-generation non-Mexican families are the comparison group. The reference person in the family is the source of information.
[2]Estimated from a linear probability regression of poverty on characteristics, where poverty equals 1 if the person is in poverty and 0 otherwise. First-generation non-Mexican persons are the comparison group.

is consistent with the income distributions shown in figure 13, where a significant percentage of third-generation Mexican American families had extremely low incomes.

The poverty rate among Mexican American individuals, however, declines with each succeeding generation. The percentage in poverty is lower for the third generation (24 percent) than for the first and second generations (both 29 percent). The third generation also has a greater percentage (64 percent) of persons with an income at least 150 percent above the poverty line than is true for the first and second generations (50 percent).

Factors Affecting Poverty Rates

The pattern of economic mobility over generations is mixed, depending on whether families or individuals are examined. It is possible that differences in individual and family characteristics explain why some are in poverty and others are not. For example, it is likely that the education level, family size, and family type of the head of the household affect how much total income all family members earn. Differences in these characteristics across generations would explain why first-generation Mexican Americans are more likely, on average, to be poor.

The bottom two sections of table 8 analyze the effect of these characteristics. Using first-generation non-Mexican-origin immigrants as the comparison group, the table shows how the family and individual poverty rates would change if Mexican American and non-Mexican immigrants had comparable levels of (1) education; (2) education and age; and (3) education, age, family size, and family type.

The adjusted poverty rates in table 8 allow us to estimate how significant each characteristic is in causing more Mexican Americans than non–Mexican Americans to be in poverty. The education and age of the head of household explains a large portion of the higher poverty rates among Mexican American families. The difference in education levels between Mexican American and non–Mexican American heads of households explains 22 to 32 percent of the poverty rate for first- and second-generation families, but only 13 percent of the rate for third-generation families. Adding age as a factor explains an additional 15 percent for first-generation Mexican American families, and an additional 4 to 7 percent for second- and third-generation families. Somewhat surprisingly, family size and family type (wife/husband-, male-, or female-headed family) explain little of the higher poverty rate among first-generation Mexican American families (an additional 5 to 6 percent for second- and third-generation families). In all, these three factors explain 41, 31, and 27 percent of the poverty rate of first-, second-, and third-generation Mexican Americans respectively. The adjusted poverty rates for Mexican American families are 16.5, 13.4, and 15.5 percent, compared to 13.3, 9.6, and 10.5 percent for non–Mexican American families.

Table 8 also examines the differences in poverty rates among individuals. After controlling for education, age, and family size and type, the poverty rates of Mexican Americans, in generational order, are 21.4, 23.1, and 17.7 percent. Mexican American individuals, especially second-generation Mexican Americans, are significantly more likely to be in poverty than is any other person with the same demographics. Lastly, even though third-generation Mexican Americans are better off than other Mexican Americans, they are not necessarily as well off as non–Mexican Americans.

Public Assistance

Antipoverty programs were implemented out of a recognition that in the majority of instances, poverty is not the fault of the individual (Schiller 1989). Prior to the Great Depression of the 1930s, the prevailing public attitude was that individuals who were poor were somehow responsible for their situation, either through action (immorality) or inaction (lack of a work ethic). But the severe economic conditions of the 1930s affected previously "moral" and "hard-working" individuals through no apparent fault of their own. For the first time, Americans began to accept that poverty was often outside a person's control. In an attempt to make America the Great Society, the Johnson administration implemented a series of antipoverty programs in the 1960s to assist the one-third of the population that was classified as poor. By 1998, 10 and 13 percent of all families and individuals, respectively, lived in poverty, a significant drop from mid-1960s levels.

Because a large percentage of the Mexican American population lives in poverty, a significant number meet the income requirements for public assistance and government welfare programs. This fact has led to a common perception that Mexican Americans are living off the taxpayers' generosity. However, the fact that a family is eligible for public assistance does not mean that they will actually receive it.

Actual statistics from public assistance and welfare programs show that Mexican American families, on average, receive more public assistance than the average non–Mexican American family. Table 9 tabulates receipt of food stamps and any other type of public assistance. The top panel shows that 2.4 percent of all Mexican American adults (age fifteen and older) received some type of public assistance in 1998, compared to 1.3 percent of the rest of the U.S. population. Second-generation non–Mexican Americans are the group least likely to receive public assistance, with less than 1 percent receiving some form of assistance. Overall, Mexican Ameri-

Table 9 Individuals Receiving Public Assistance or Food Stamps, by Generation

	First	Second	Third	Total
PERSONS RECEIVING PUBLIC ASSISTANCE				
Mexican American				
Total persons	159,874	66,489	105,608	331,971
Percent of generation	2.4%	2.4%	2.5%	2.4%
Adjusted percent (for poverty and age)[1]	−0.1%	1.1%	0.9%	1.2%
Non–Mexican American				
Total persons	305,039	106,414	2,077,446	2,488,899
Percent of generation	1.7%	0.7%	1.3%	1.3%
Adjusted percent (for poverty and age)[1]	0.5%	0.7%	0.6%	1.3%
HOUSEHOLDS IN WHICH ANY MEMBER RECEIVED FOOD STAMPS				
Mexican American				
Total households	313,755	105,453	250,425	669,632
Percent of generation	11.7%	10.8%	14.4%	12.4%
Adjusted percent (for poverty and age)[2]	3.6%	6.2%	8.8%	7.5%
Non–Mexican American				
Total households	519,237	215,554	4,700,375	545,166
Percent of generation	6.2%	2.8%	5.8%	5.6%
Adjusted percent (for poverty and age)[2]	2.9%	2.8%	4.0%	5.6%

Source: Author's weighted tabulations from the March 1999 Current Population Survey.

Note: Excludes persons under age sixteen or unrelated to the family.

[1]Estimated from a linear probability regression of public assistance status on generation, Mexican origin, age, and poverty. The omitted category is second-generation non–Mexican Americans, except in the Total category, where all non–Mexican Americans are the omitted group and no controls for generation are included.

[2]Estimated from a linear probability regression of whether anyone in the household received food stamps on generation, Mexican origin, age, and poverty. One observation per household. The omitted category is second-generation non–Mexican Americans, except in the Total category, where all non–Mexican Americans are the omitted group, and no controls for generation are included.

can families are two times as likely to receive public assistance as their non-Mexican-origin counterparts. In addition, Mexican American households are more than twice as likely to receive food stamps compared to the non-Mexican-origin U.S. population.

A possible explanation for the fact that a higher percentage of Mexican Americans receives welfare is because they are poorer and younger than the rest of the population. Although other factors come into play, it is instructive to examine the extent to which these two factors explain the difference in participation rates. The adjusted percent rows adjust for poverty and age relative to second-generation non–Mexican Americans. Once poverty rates and age are equalized, Mexican Americans are slightly less likely to participate in public assistance programs (1.2 percent) than is the rest of the population (1.3 percent).

Surprisingly, once age and poverty differences are eliminated, first-generation Mexican Americans—that is, immigrants—are less likely to receive public assistance than any other group including second-generation Americans, with less than 1 percent participating in public assistance programs. (The negative sign in table 9 is an artifact of the statistical procedure used.) This conclusion is supported by Tienda and Liang (1994), who estimate that less than 2 and 5 percent (unadjusted) of legalized and **undocumented Mexican immigrants,** respectively, received AFDC (Aid to Families with Dependent Children) and food stamps in 1987. (U.S.–born children of undocumented immigrants are eligible for AFDC and food stamps.) Both of these percentages were significantly lower than those for the rest of the U.S. population.

This finding is exactly the opposite of what supporters of anti-immigration laws, such as California's Proposition 187, claim. Jesse Laguna (1994), for example, states that immigrants come to the United States mostly for the welfare benefits. Clearly this is not the case, given the low number of immigrants that receive assistance (about 160,000). Even though the adjusted participation rates for second- and third-generation Mexican Americans are still higher than those for other Americans, these rates are more than 50 percent lower than the non-adjusted rates. Thus, as Mexican Americans grow older and earn more, it is predicted that they will participate less and less in welfare programs. Accounting for additional differences between Mexican Americans and other Americans (such as education levels) would undoubtedly further reduce the gap.

Once poverty and age differences between Mexican American and non-Mexican-origin households are eliminated, participation rates in the food stamp program become much more similar between the two groups. First-generation Mexican American households have nearly the same participation rate (3.6 percent) as first- and second-generation non–Mexican American households (2.9 and 2.8 percent respectively); however, second- and third-generation Mexican Americans have higher adjusted rates than other U.S. households. Poverty and age explain about 40 to 69 percent of the higher participation by Mexican American households.

■ The Underclass Model

The statistics on income, poverty, and public assistance paint a somewhat bleak picture of Mexican Americans in the American economy and society. The underclass model argues that a shortage of high-paying, year-round employment opportunities; declining marriage rates; residential concentration in barrios; and lack of positive role models create a cycle of poverty (Mincy 1994). This cycle of poverty is difficult to break out of, resulting in generation after generation being mired in poverty. This hypothesis was originally popularized in application to black Americans, but sometimes it has also been applied to other urban poor populations including Latinos, especially Puerto Ricans (Chapa 1988; Hayes-Bautista 1996; Mincy 1994; Moore 1989; Vélez-Ibáñez 1993).

According to one definition, an underclass consists of individuals and families "who lack training and skills and either experience long-term unemployment or are not members of the labor force . . . are engaged in street crime and other forms of aberrant behavior, and . . . experience long-term spells of poverty and/or welfare dependency" (William Julius Wilson, quoted in Mincy 1994, 123). Although this definition avoids racial or cultural explanations for poverty, politicians, journalists, and others sometimes misapply the underclass hypothesis and claim that poverty results from cultural deficiency. That is, blacks and Mexican Americans are poor because they are lazy, drug addicts, criminally inclined, and prefer government support over work because their culture does not value accomplishment and the Puritan work ethic (Mincy 1994). The terms *poverty* and *underclass* are often confused, but it is important to distinguish between the two, especially in the Mexican American and Hispanic community. Poverty is a measure of current income relative to a government-defined, dollar-based standard of living, whereas underclass implies enduring conditions that extend beyond income—a permanent "ghetto-specific culture" that is characterized by lack of economic and social mobility, either by choice or because of structural barriers (Mincy 1994; Moore 1989).

Attempts to answer the question of whether Mexican Americans constitute an underclass have relied on socioeconomic indicators. Several researchers—including Chapa (1988, 1989–90), Chapa and Valencia (1993), and Rochin and de la Torre (1996)—have concluded that Mexican Americans are not likely to make economic progress, either within their lifetimes or across generations. These authors point to a variety of evidence, including the lack of change in poverty rates, growing income inequality between Hispanics and non-Hispanic whites, growth of female-headed households, higher **unemployment rates**, and lack of occupational mobility. However, evidence for their conclusions is not based on an intergenerational and interethnic analysis of poverty rates, income growth, or educational growth. Some of these studies, moreover, have failed to separate newly arrived immigrants from established immigrants or second- and higher-generation Mexican Americans, although Trejo (1997), Chapa (1988), and Chapa (1989–90) are exceptions to this generalization. It is also possible that Mexican Americans may differ from other Americans in systematic ways that may account for their seemingly intractable lower **socioeconomic status.** If these differences do explain the higher poverty rates of Mexican Americans, policies can be implemented to deal with the causes rather than the symptoms of poverty or underclass status.

In her review of Mexican American economic studies, Moore (1989, 277) concludes that "few of the poor Hispanic communities studied display the features . . . defined as 'underclass' " but nevertheless this "should not be grounds for complacency." Additional evidence that poor Mexican Americans do not fit the traditional profile of those stuck in poverty is provided by Chávez (1991), Gutkind (1986), and Rodríguez (1996). Gutkind questions the notion that there is only one type of poor person. The perception that all poor people are alike leads to beliefs such as, "**Chicanos** are lazy and will never get anywhere" (Gutkind 1986, 191). At a minimum, he identifies eight groups within the poor: including the "Chicana doer" (who attempts to escape poverty despite limited resources by investing in education or saving her earnings) and "young Chicanos."

Chicanos merit two subgroups because their positive attitudes toward work, family, their community, and their future prospects (in terms of education, work, and other aspects of society) distinguish them from other groups in poverty. Despite the immediate problems in their neighborhoods and other economic troubles, the majority of poor Mexican Americans have positive attitudes toward work and school, and plan for the future. Health status is another area where Mexican Americans differ from other populations in poverty. On average, the health status of Mexican American women is very good. They eat a balanced diet and avoid excessive drinking, smoking, or drug use (Abraído-Lanza et al. 1999).

These characteristics contrast with the classical profile of the poor, who tend to be poor because either they do not look for work or they work for limited periods to satisfy an immediate desire. These individuals perceive themselves as unable to advance out of their situation. As a consequence of these psychological characteristics, their aspirations for the future are very low, which in turn creates a cycle of poverty that justifies lack of participation in the labor market and other institutions (Chávez 1991; Rodríguez 1996).

Chávez (1991) and Rodríguez (1996), among others, also challenge the stereotypes that most Hispanics are poor and permanently disadvantaged persons, and more importantly that there are few middle-class Latinos. Rodríguez (1996, 6) argues that Latinos comprise a significant share of the middle class, and that there are a significant number of "Latino families improving their lot and achieving their 'American dream.'" Both Chávez and Rodríguez claim the majority of Hispanics are in the process of acculturating and, therefore, should not be expected to have the same socioeconomic status as long-established ethnic groups. Chávez, for example, points out that in the early twentieth century other immigrant groups started out at the bottom of the socioeconomic ladder, but they have now attained equal status with long-established ethnic groups.

Defining what constitutes the middle class is difficult. One possible definition is to use the *median value of per capita household income* as the cutoff point for the middle class. In 1998, this amount was $16,203 (note that this figure is per individual family member, not for the entire household). Using a per capita measure, rather than aggregate household income, is preferable because it factors out differences in household size. Rodríguez (1996) extends the definition of middle-class households to include homeownership, a feature also adopted here.

Table 10 compares the number and percentage of Mexican American and non–Mexican American households that fall into the middle class. The working definition of middle class used in table 10 is households with a per capita income of at least $16,203 or who own their home. Using this definition, the majority (56.6 percent) of Mexican American households are middle class. Despite their low education level, initially low English ability, and other factors, nearly half of first-generation Mexican Americans fall into the middle class. By the second generation, 68.5 percent are in the middle class, an increase of more than 40 percent. In comparison, for non–Mexican Americans the increase is only 30 percent, indicating that Mexican American households have greater movement into the middle class. Consistent

Table 10 Number and Percentage of Middle-Class Households, by Generation

	First	Second	Third	Total
MEXICAN AMERICAN				
Number of households	2,689,799	976,850	1,735,186	5,401,835
Percent	48.7%	68.5%	63.6%	56.6%
Adjusted percent[1]	73.7%	83.4%	78.9%	72.5%
NON–MEXICAN AMERICAN				
Number of households	8,345,903	7,625,126	80,915,910	96,886,938
Percent	66.0%	85.3%	82.3%	81.2%
Adjusted percent[1]	73.0%	85.3%	88.2%	81.2%

Source: Author's weighted tabulations from the March 1999 Current Population Survey.
Notes: Middle class is defined as having at least a per capita income of $16,203 and/or owning a home. Excludes those in group quarters.
[1]The adjusted poverty rates factor in age, Mexican origin, generation, and education level of the head of household in a linear probability regression of middle-class status. The omitted category is second-generation non–Mexican Americans, except in the Total category, where all non–Mexican Americans are the omitted group and no controls for generation are included.

with the pattern that recurs throughout the measures in this chapter, a smaller percentage of the third generation is in the middle class compared to the second generation. This pattern holds for both Mexican Americans (63.6 percent) and non-Mexican-origin households (82.3 percent).

Factoring out differences in education and age between Mexican American and non-Mexican-origin heads of households helps explain why there is a smaller percentage of middle-class Mexican Americans. For each generation, a higher percentage of Mexican Americans would be expected to be in the middle class if these heads of households had the same age and education as second-generation non–Mexican Americans. Thus, if age and education levels were equal between the two groups, 73.7 percent of first-generation Mexican American households and 73.0 percent of first-generation non-Mexican-origin households would be classified as middle class. The adjusted rates for the second and third generations are 83.4 and 78.9 percent for Mexican Americans and 85.3 and 88.2 percent for non–Mexican Americans.

Evidence that Mexican Americans gradually have improved their situation is also provided by DeFreitas (1991). He notes that changes in the macroeconomy—such as a decrease in industrial employment, economic recessions, and Mexican American migration from rural areas to urban areas in the Southwest after 1945—contributed to a decline in poverty rates among U.S.–born and foreign-born Mexicans. Whereas in 1949 Mexican immigrants had a poverty rate of about 40 percent, making them the poorest Hispanic group, by 1979 this rate had decreased to nearly 25 percent; Puerto Ricans are now the poorest Hispanic group.

The income and poverty information provided in tables 7 to 10 shows that progress seems to stall for some third-generation Mexican Americans, as it does for non–Mexican Americans as well. To allow for a more detailed comparison with other ethnic groups, table 11 presents income and poverty rates for Mexican American, non-Hispanic white, black, other Hispanic (non-Mexican), and Asian families. Every ethnic group has higher poverty rates in the third generation than the second. Furthermore, only among Asians and Mexicans does the third generation have a higher mean income than the second generation. Whereas whites, blacks, and non-Mexican Hispanics have significantly lower incomes in the third generation, third-generation Mexican Americans have higher mean ($43,346) and median ($34,000) incomes than their second-generation counterparts ($41,270 and $30,800, respectively).

It is surprising that the second generation does better because one would expect more acculturated generations to be more familiar with American institutions and therefore to have better socioeconomic outcomes than earlier generations. A possible explanation for the better socioeconomic performance of the second generation is their immigrant heritage. Kao and Tienda (1995), for example, argue that the sons and daughters of immigrants perform better scholastically than do students whose parents are born in the United States because immigrants transmit immigrant optimism—that is, values, aspirations, and optimism about their prospects for the future. These characteristics result in a high-achieving second generation. Unfortunately, the implication is that the third generation has relatively lower levels of motivation and drive. The patterns observed in the tables support this hypothesis. It may be that the "stalled progress" observed for Mexican Americans is simply part of a process that all ethnic groups undergo. From this point of view, **acculturation** and **assimilation** actually have some negative side effects.

The consensus among studies of the impact of acculturation is that there is evidence of progress and improvement (Chávez 1991; Hayes-Bautista 1996; Moore 1989; Rodríguez 1996; Trejo 1997). Studies by Chávez (1991), DeFreitas (1991), and Trejo (1997), as well as the data presented in this book not only account for a portion of the socioeconomic disparities with

Table 11 Family Income and Poverty Rates, by Generation and Ethnicity

	FIRST		SECOND		THIRD		TOTAL	
	Mean	Median	Mean	Median	Mean	Median	Mean	Median
MEXICAN AMERICAN								
Income	$32,358	$25,000	$41,270	$30,800	$43,346	$34,000	$37,277	$27,600
Percent in poverty	28.1%	—	19.4%	—	21.2%	—	24.5%	—
NON-HISPANIC WHITE								
Income	$72,281	$51,328	$68,495	$49,718	$64,629	$51,492	$65,239	$51,360
Percent in poverty	9.3%	—	3.8%	—	6.2%	—	6.1%	—
BLACK								
Income	$38,521	$33,280	$46,516	$35,526	$38,423	$28,982	$38,528	$38,528
Percent in poverty	22.3%	—	10.4%	—	23.5%	—	23.3%	—
OTHER HISPANIC (NON-MEXICAN)								
Income	$42,957	$31,147	$58,457	$47,019	$47,884	$39,000	$45,433	$34,004
Percent in poverty	18.9%	—	10.1%	—	15.4%	—	17.4%	—
ASIAN								
Income	$67,562	$51,110	$65,708	$60,017	$79,289	$65,885	$68,714	$54,000
Percent in poverty	11.2%	—	3.5%	—	9.5%	—	10.4%	—

Source: Author's weighted tabulations from the March 1999 Current Population Survey.
Note: Only primary families are counted.

non-Hispanic whites, but also document the ongoing progress of Mexican Americans. It is clear, however, that they have not yet attained parity despite the progress made by second- and third-generation U.S. residents. Many of the economic disparities between Mexican Americans and non-Hispanic whites can be explained by differences in education, age, and other demographic characteristics, such as English ability, that are correlated with acculturation. Therefore, parity in the wider socioeconomic sense should be achieved if differences in these underlying demographic variables are eliminated.

Wealth and Asset Accumulation

Sources of income outside of wages are assets and **wealth**. Examples of assets are homes, cars, jewelry, stocks, and bonds; and wealth is defined as

Table 12 Asset Accumulation, by Generation

	First	Second	Third	Total
HOMEOWNERSHIP				
Mexican American	41.7%	59.2%	52.6%	48.4%
Non–Mexican American	49.3%	73.2%	69.5%	68.1%
DIVIDEND INCOME				
Mexican American				
Total dividend recipients	2.5%	11.3%	12.1%	7.2%
Non–middle-class recipients	0.3%	3.7%	4.7%	1.9%
Recipients in middle class and above	4.9%	14.7%	16.4%	11.2%
Mean value of dividends	$3,662	$2,690	$1,986	$2,508
Non–Mexican American				
Total dividend recipients	22.3%	35.0%	30.3%	30.0%
Non–middle-class recipients	5.1%	9.2%	6.9%	6.8%
Recipients in middle class and above	31.1%	39.5%	35.4%	35.4%
Mean value of dividends	$4,556	$6,212	$4,229	$4,433

Source: Author's weighted tabulations from the March 1999 Current Population Survey.
Notes: Householders are the unit of observation. See table 10 for the definition of middle class. Excludes those in group quarters.

the total value of these assets. Wealth is different from wage income because the latter represents the value of a person's productivity at a particular point in time, say the previous two weeks of work. In contrast, wealth is the value of all the material goods owned by the individual in both the present and future. Assets are often considered more important than current income because they can be used as collateral to obtain credit or loans and because they include value over a longer period of time (such as future Social Security receipts). In addition, assets create economic security for current and future generations because they can be passed from one generation to the next.

Table 12 examines the percentage of persons who have assets, as measured by homeownership and dividend income (payment from stocks or investments). Homeownership and stocks are long-established measures of assets, but they are not perfect measures of all aspects of wealth. For example, one homeowner may have a house worth $500,000 whereas another may own a home worth $50,000. Nevertheless, homeownership and stock ownership are measures of economic activity that are highly correlated with wealth and asset accumulation.

Nearly half of all Mexican American heads of households are home-

Buying a home can be difficult process even for native-born, English-speaking persons. Multiple factors have limited the ability of many Latinos to purchase a home. In the 1990s, however, various home-purchase programs around the country enabled more Latinos to become home-owners. Buying a home is a dream come true for many of them.

Brothers Javier and Rafael Mendoza, immigrants from central Mexico who work as siding contractors, bought houses last year in the Seattle area. Javier and his wife bought their home first because they were able to qualify quickly, once their job histories and credit from Mexico were approved. For Rafael and his wife, Mary, it took about six months to get their finances in order. Raphael said, "We are here a few years, in an apartment. We don't think we can ever buy a house. We don't know people. No credit. Not much money. We did not know what to do." Through their real estate agent, they found out about a first-time home buyers' seminar in Spanish. Similar workshops offered by community organizations and the Department of Housing and Urban Development are facilitating the process for individuals who have never purchased a home.

Builders and lenders are not only increasing their bilingual staff through a national Hispanic Initiative, they are also doing more marketing directed at Latinos, such as advertising in Spanish-language newspapers and target-ing buyers at flea markets. Other lenders are putting out slick multilingual advertisements to attract Latinos.

More flexible lending standards instituted during the recession in the early 1990s spurred the increase in Latino homeownership. Qualifi-cation requirements have been eased and down payments have dropped from the traditional 10 or 20 percent to 5 percent, 3 percent, or even nothing.

Immigrants usually spend a decade or more either living with relatives or renting before they can purchase their own home. Often Latinos will join with family or friends to buy their first home, and lenders are now more willing to make such multiple-party loans. "Sometimes you'll have two couples buy a three- or four-bedroom home," said María Camerena, a Realtor in Los Angeles. "Usually the intention is to stay together for a couple of years until the other couple can buy them out."

The Federal National Mortgage Association, known as Fannie Mae, is the federally chartered funding source for issuers of mortgages. It has adopted policies allowing lenders to use alternate forms of credit—such as rent stubs or phone bills—to help establish a buyer's credit record.

Two federal acts have also contributed to the increase in Latino home-ownership. A Clinton administration directive to strengthen the 1977 Community Reinvestment Act, the nation's major anti-discrimination law in lending, has provided more opportunities for people of color. Enacted in 1975 and expanded in 1989, the Home Mortgage Disclosure Act (HMDA) requires strict loan reporting standards, and as a consequence has reduced discrimination against prospective Latino home buyers. (From Hevesi 1999; Lee 1998; O'Neill 1994; Reiner 1994)

owners. The homeownership rate is lowest among first-generation house-holders (41.7 percent) and highest among the second generation (59.2 percent). In total, Mexican American householders are 20 percentage points less likely than other Americans to own a home, but this difference is lowest among the first generation (about 8 points).

Recent trends, however, suggest that Mexican Americans, especially immigrants, are buying homes at a faster pace than non-Hispanic whites. Despite the economic recession of the early 1990s, Latinos purchased homes in record numbers, while maintaining lower than average mortgage default rates. At a time when declining home values and economic uncertainty were scaring away many potential homebuyers, many Mexican Americans took advantage of relaxed lending rules to purchase homes (Lee 1998). For the first time, these new Latino homeowners felt a sense of long-term economic security.

Armida Hernández, a new homeowner, says "We're trying to provide some kind of future for our son so that maybe when he goes to college he'll have something he can sell to cover his expenses," (O'Neill 1994). Despite the younger, poorer, and less-acculturated profile of the Mexican American population, it is likely that more of them will be fulfilling part of the American dream.

The other indicator of wealth—dividend income—shows that Mexican Americans are significantly less likely than non–Mexican Americans to own stocks, mutual funds, and other assets that yield dividends. In all, 7.2 percent of Mexican American householders report receiving dividend income, in contrast to 30.0 percent of non-Mexican-origin householders. For both populations, middle-class households are significantly more likely than poorer households to receive dividend income. Less than 2 percent of all non-middle-class Mexican American households receive dividend income, compared to slightly more than 11 percent of all middle-class Mexican Americans. (Note that the definition of middle class includes the wealthy.) Compared to non–Mexican Americans of the same class, however, Mexican Americans are significantly less likely to receive dividend income. Some explanations for the lower average rates of participation include lower average income, language barriers, lack of a tradition of investment in Latin American countries, mistrust of financial institutions, and a failure by financial institutions to reach out aggressively to the Mexican American population, either through direct campaigns or by hiring more Hispanics with insights into the community (Domínguez 1999). Yet, table 12 indicates that participation in the stock market increases with each succeeding generation of Mexican Americans (from 5 to 16 percent for the middle class and 0 to 5 percent for those below middle class). The increase in participation between the second and third generations is the opposite of the pattern observed among the rest of U.S. households and contradicts the general pattern seen in other measures of socioeconomic status.

The value of all assets is also significantly lower for Mexican American than for non-Mexican-origin households, with an average value of about $2,500 for the former and $4,400 for the latter. Interestingly enough, dividend income falls from one generation to the next among Mexican Americans. One possible explanation is that first- and second-generation householders who own assets are older than third-generation householders and therefore have accumulated more assets. Furthermore, the type of assets owned may also account for the lower dividend income. For example, younger individuals are more likely to invest in riskier investments that fluctuate in value, so even if they own the same number of stocks and bonds as first- or second-generation individuals, they may receive less dividend income.

Recognizing the $350 billion purchasing power of Hispanics, various financial institutions have recently initiated outreach efforts to this population. If these campaigns are implemented thoughtfully and carried out over a prolonged period of time, the prospects are good that a larger share of Mexican Americans will buy more of the U.S. economy—and hence command more of its fruits (Domínguez 1999).

◼ Summary

Mexican Americans are one of the poorest ethnic groups in the country. At the same time, their lower income is largely due to generational status— each succeeding generation has higher average and median incomes. This is a departure from the pattern observed for non-Mexican-origin households, which experience lower incomes in the third generation than in the second. In addition, the higher poverty rate among Mexican Americans can be explained largely by differences in their education, age, family size, and family type.

As a direct consequence of the low income and poverty that characterize Mexican Americans, they are more likely than other U.S. residents to participate in public assistance programs. Still, the numbers of Mexican Americans receiving assistance is relatively low. In addition, their participation is largely influenced not only by poverty, but also by age as well as other factors not directly examined here. Considering the higher poverty rates of Mexican Americans, a smaller percentage of those eligible utilize public assistance than is true for other groups.

Participation in government assistance programs is one characteristic associated with a permanent underclass. However, given their lower-than-expected adjusted participation rates, their work ethic, and their family values, the underclass model is not applicable to Mexican Americans. Mexican Americans are poor, but the evidence suggests upward, albeit slow, mobility.

The acquisition of assets is another area where Mexican Americans trail other Americans, although homeownership is one area where Mexican Americans are making significant inroads. Lower income, youthfulness, and difficulty in accessing financial institutions are the primary reasons why Mexican Americans have fewer assets than the average American. As more Mexican Americans join the ranks of the middle class and are solicited by financial institutions, this difference is expected to diminish.

Will Mexican Americans reach parity with non-Hispanic whites or Asians? Unfortunately, it is impossible to answer this question because the majority are descendants of immigrants who are still climbing the socioeconomic ladder. The evidence found among present-day Mexican Americans suggests that they have not stopped climbing that ladder, however. The challenge for Mexican Americans is to keep reaching for the next rung in the climb toward *buenos días*.

■ Discussion Questions

1. Describe the change in income from the first to the third generation for Mexican Americans and non–Mexican Americans.

2. Why do some third-generation Mexican American families have lower income levels than second-generation families?

3. What factors are considered in the definition of poverty? How is poverty different from standard of living?

4. What roles do education and age play in the poverty rate among Mexican American families?

5. What is the underclass model? Is this model applicable to Mexican Americans? Why or why not?

6. How does the accumulation of assets among Mexican Americans compare to that among non–Mexican Americans? Discuss the importance of homeownership to Mexican Americans in light of their increasing homeownership rates.

■ Suggested Readings

Chapa, Jorge. 1989–90. The Myth of Hispanic Progress: Trends in the Educational and Economic Attainment of Mexican Americans. *Journal of Hispanic Policy* 4, 3–18.

Chávez, Linda 1991. *Out of the Barrio: Toward a New Politics of Hispanic Assimilation.* New York: Basic Books.

DeFreitas, Gregory. 1991. *Inequality at Work: Hispanics in the U.S. Labor Force.* New York: Oxford University Press.

Gutkind, Efraim. 1986. *Patterns of Economic Behaviour among the American Poor.* London: Macmillan.

Hayes-Bautista, David. 1996. Poverty and the Underclass: Some Latino Crosscurrents. In *Reducing Poverty in America: Views and Approaches,* edited by Michael R. Darby. Thousand Oaks, Calif.: Sage.

Moore, Joan. 1989. Is There a Hispanic Underclass? *Social Science Quarterly* 70, 265–85.

6

Trabajando

MEXICAN AMERICANS IN THE LABOR MARKET

Gerardo "Lalo" Medina was the road manager for Ozomatli, one of the more exciting and innovative music groups, as well as the tour manager for Dilated Peoples and Jurassic 5, both Los Angeles–based underground hip-hop groups. Medina was responsible for the everyday activities of the bands, from ensuring that their hotel reservations were correct to making sure that they made it to the next city on time to set up and prepare for the next show. He said "My job was to ensure the entire tour ran smoothly. This meant dealing with all details, large and small, and handling all the finances on the road. I was Daddy, Mommy, and friend." Medina did not set out to be a road and tour manager when he graduated from college. He graduated with a bachelor's degree from the University of California at Riverside and was an English teacher in Southern California. During this time, he was also involved in various creative activities, including contributions to the political satire group Pocho. Despite the monetary uncertainty of working in the entertainment industry, Medina thinks that the opportunities are worth the risks. The rewards have paid off: he has used his liberal arts education as well as his life experiences to make the bands' various tours successful ones—the bands consistently sell out their shows and leave a trail of happy concert-goers in their wake.

In order to understand the underlying factors affecting the economic mobility, or lack thereof, of Mexican Americans, it is necessary to understand the labor market position of Mexican Americans, including unemployment, wages, and occupational status. This examination is the final component in the economic profile of Mexican Americans.

Workers provide their time to employers in the production of a service or product in exchange for some compensation, usually in the form of money. The labor market is comprised of all these elements: workers, employers, and the compensation workers receive for the labor they provide. Economic theory suggests that workers who acquire skills or knowledge are more productive. Furthermore, workers who are highly productive in some measurable way will earn more because they are more valuable to employers.

In this chapter, only the supply side of the labor market is examined; that is, the labor market activity and wages of workers. In addition to providing a general portrait of Mexican American workers, it explains their various labor market outcomes. In keeping with the overall theme, the chapter provides evidence that shows an improvement in the status of Mexican Americans from one generation to the next.

Labor economists measure labor supply in different ways, including **labor force participation** (LFP, also termed *labor force attachment*) and the number of hours worked during a specific amount of time, such as a week or a year. The amount of income earned by workers is also of considerable interest, and much effort is devoted to understanding why workers earn the amount they do. Therefore, this chapter profiles these different areas of the labor market for Mexican Americans.

■ Labor Market Activity

Activity in the labor market can take different forms, including **part-time** and **full-time** work, entry into and out of the labor market, search for employment, and the type of occupation workers are employed in. The majority of the working-age population not enrolled in school (that is, individuals sixteen to sixty-four years old) has two options with regard to the labor market: participate or not. Labor force participants are people who have a paying job or are looking for one. Therefore, LFP includes all unemployed people, because an unemployed person is defined as someone without a job but actively looking for one. The definition of LFP excludes workers who do not receive compensation for their labor, such as family members who work in a family business for free or persons who volunteer their time to charitable organizations. Other individuals not participating in the labor force include those who wish not to work and those unable to work, such as persons with a physical disability, for example.

Table 13 presents labor market activity during the first week of March 1999. The four possible outcomes for an individual eligible to be in the labor force are as follows: non-participation in the labor force, full-time work, part-time work, or unemployment. The total number of Mexican

Table 13 Labor Force Activity, by Generation and Gender, March 1999

	MALE				FEMALE			
	First	Second	Third	Total	First	Second	Third	Total
MEXICAN AMERICAN								
Not in labor force	7.8%	13.2%	12.8%	10.0%	50.6%	29.1%	27.1%	39.2%
Work full time	81.4%	76.2%	75.3%	78.9%	35.1%	50.7%	53.6%	43.8%
Work part time	6.1%	6.1%	6.4%	6.2%	9.6%	13.9%	14.4%	11.9%
Unemployed	4.7%	4.5%	5.5%	4.9%	4.7%	6.3%	4.9%	5.1%
Total labor force (in 1,000s)	3,236	833	1,591	5,660	2,637	921	1,704	5,263
NON-HISPANIC WHITE								
Not in labor force	11.0%	13.9%	10.9%	11.1%	34.2%	27.7%	24.9%	25.4%
Work full time	76.8%	75.7%	80.9%	80.4%	49.4%	51.8%	57.0%	56.5%
Work part time	6.9%	6.8%	5.3%	5.4%	13.7%	18.2%	15.9%	16.0%
Unemployed	5.3%	3.6%	3.0%	3.1%	2.7%	2.2%	2.2%	2.2%
Total labor force (in 1,000s)	2,235	2,890	50,122	55,247	2,253	2,866	51,212	56,331
BLACK								
Not in labor force	13.2%	27.4%	22.7%	22.0%	26.1%	25.1%	24.7%	24.8%
Work full time	79.5%	56.9%	64.8%	65.8%	56.8%	54.9%	59.0%	58.8%
Work part time	4.7%	10.9%	5.7%	5.7%	9.4%	13.8%	10.6%	10.6%
Unemployed	2.6%	4.8%	6.8%	6.5%	7.8%	6.2%	5.7%	5.8%
Total labor force (in 1,000s)	674	134	7,581	8,389	644	148	9,419	10,212
OTHER HISPANIC								
Not in labor force	10.5%	13.7%	17.4%	12.1%	35.7%	18.7%	29.0%	32.7%
Work full time	79.4%	69.2%	72.1%	76.8%	47.5%	63.5%	54.1%	50.3%
Work part time	5.2%	9.0%	5.7%	5.8%	13.1%	13.7%	13.6%	13.3%
Unemployed	4.9%	8.2%	4.8%	5.3%	3.7%	4.2%	3.2%	3.6%
Total labor force (in 1,000s)	1,612	300	383	2,295	1,877	283	429	2,589
ASIAN								
Not in labor force	13.4%	11.1%	11.6%	13.0%	33.6%	26.2%	21.7%	31.8%
Work full time	78.2%	72.3%	77.0%	77.6%	52.4%	57.9%	63.4%	54.0%
Work part time	5.9%	11.3%	7.3%	6.5%	11.7%	13.3%	11.4%	11.8%
Unemployed	2.5%	5.4%	4.1%	2.9%	2.3%	2.5%	3.5%	2.4%
Total labor force (in 1,000s)	2,254	220	325	2,799	2,565	236	330	3,130

Source: Author's weighted tabulations from the March 1999 Current Population Survey.

Notes: Includes persons age sixteen to sixty-four and not attending school, living in group quarters, or serving in the armed forces.

American workers is 10.8 million, of which 5.7 million are men and 5.3 million are women.

One of the most revealing aspects of the labor activity of Mexican American workers is the fact that Mexican American men have the highest LFP rates in the country, with 90 percent working or looking for work, compared to 87 and 89 percent of Asian and non-Hispanic white men, respectively.

Full-time work is defined as working thirty-five or more hours per week, and part-time work as working fewer than thirty-five hours a week. Although full-time work is not necessarily the preferred type of employment, first- and second-generation Mexican American males have the highest percentage of full-time workers in their respective generations of any ethnic group (81.4 and 76.2 percent). Furthermore, third-generation Mexican Americans have the third-highest percentage of full-time workers after non-Hispanic whites and Asians. These LFP rates are consistent with those given in other studies (Borjas 1982; Borjas and Tienda 1985; DeFreitas 1985, 1991).

On the other hand, part-time employment is not a significant source of employment for Mexican American males, as only 6 percent work part time. Although this percentage is the second highest among all working men, it is not out of the ordinary compared to other groups.

In contrast to the high LFP rates of men, Mexican American women have the lowest rates of participation among women, with nearly 40 percent not being in the labor force. This is especially true among immigrant women, more than half of whom are not in the labor force. A much higher percentage of second- and third-generation Mexican American women, more than 70 percent, either work or are looking for work. Therefore, the immigrant experience, or perhaps the culture associated with the immigrant generation, is a significant factor in Mexican American females' decision about whether or not to seek employment (Segura 1992).

Yet, compared to other second- or third-generation women, Mexican American women are still less likely to be labor force participants. These generations of women in most other ethnic groups have LFP rates of around 75 percent. Non-Mexican Hispanic and white women have rates similar to these generations of Mexican American women.

Compared to men, a larger percentage of Mexican American working women have part-time jobs. Table 13 shows that 10 to 14 percent of Mexican American women work part time. Overall, table 13 shows that only

Table 14 Average Number of Weeks Spent Looking for Work in 1998

	MALE				FEMALE			
	First	Second	Third	Total	First	Second	Third	Total
Mexican American	8.6	7.7	8.6	8.5	6.3	7.3	7.5	6.9
Non-Hispanic white	5.7	6.4	7.4	7.3	4.3	3.8	4.2	4.2
Black	15.4	16.6	11.3	11.7	4.2	6.0	8.5	8.3
Other Hispanic	8.6	5.8	8.5	8.5	7.2	4.3	4.0	6.6
Asian	5.9	7.2	10.1	7.2	3.1	10.2	4.8	4.0

Source: Author's weighted tabulations from the March 1999 Current Population Survey.
Notes: Includes persons age sixteen to sixty-four and not attending school, living in group quarters, or serving in the armed forces. Includes those who worked for part of 1998 as well as those who did not work but looked for work.

white and non-Mexican Hispanic women are more likely to have part-time jobs than Mexican American women, a pattern also reported by Reimers (1992). Combined with the low labor force attachment of Mexican American women, the use of part-time employment suggests a strategic use of the labor market by Mexican American women and families (Segura 1992). That is, it is possible that Mexican American women balance economic issues with domestic and cultural expectations by working only part time. It could also be that Mexican American women have more difficulty finding work, as demonstrated by their high **unemployment rate** and by the greater number of weeks it takes them to find a job (see table 14).

Unfortunately, one reason why Mexican Americans have a strong labor force attachment is their high unemployment rate. Table 13 shows that Mexican Americans have unemployment rates between 5 and 6 percent, whereas whites and Asians have rates ranging from 2 to 5 percent. Only blacks have higher unemployment rates (6 percent or higher), and other Hispanics have somewhat comparable rates. High levels of unemployment may result from difficulty in finding a new job after losing one or from a higher frequency of job loss. DeFreitas (1985) finds evidence that the problem of unemployment lies in the duration, rather than the frequency, of unemployment: the unemployment rate for Mexican Americans is affected nearly twice as much by an inability to find a job than by the loss of a job. Table 14 supports this finding and shows that, on average, Mexican Americans spend more weeks than non-Hispanic whites looking for a job, although not as many as black workers do. Nevertheless, the 1.2 extra weeks spent by all Mexican American males and the 2.7 extra weeks spent by Mexican American females means that, relative to whites, Mexican Americans who lose their jobs are going to be unemployed for a longer time.

■ Employment Patterns

Contrary to the stereotype of the "lazy Mexican" (Monroy 1999), Mexican Americans have a very strong work ethic as shown by their labor force activity. Table 15 provides further evidence that the work ethic and labor force attachment of Mexican Americans are higher than or at least comparable to those of other ethnic groups. Among the employed, the number of weeks worked during the year and the number of hours worked per week are indicative of how much workers work. Table 15 shows that, on average, Mexican American men work the second fewest number of weeks and hours per week of all ethnic groups (less than forty-eight weeks and forty-two hours per week), but the number of hours worked per week is only 0.7 hours less than the average for the other groups. Likewise Mexican American women work the fewest number of weeks of any group of women but work a similar number of hours per week. Thus, although a high percentage of Mexican Americans work, their longer unemployment spells reduce the number of weeks and hours they are able to work.

The ability to find and maintain a full-time job, defined as thirty-five or more hours per week year-round, is also an indicator of success and stability in the labor market. Although many individuals choose not to work full time, most workers are seeking full-time work. Table 16 examines the percentage of workers aged sixteen to sixty-four who worked full time. Among men, Mexican Americans have the second lowest percentage of year-round, full-time workers, barely ahead of blacks. In all, 71.9 percent of all Mexican American men were working full time, compared to 76.2 percent of non-Hispanic white men.

First-generation Mexican American males are the least likely immigrant group to work full-time year-round. This low percentage most likely is the result of low education and employment in occupations that are seasonal in nature. The second generation has an even lower percentage of full-time, year-round workers (67.4 percent), but this percentage is the second highest among all second-generation male workers. Similarly, the percentage of full-time, year-round workers is lower for third-generation

Table 15 Average Number of Weeks and Hours per Week Worked in 1998, by Generation

	MALE				FEMALE			
	First	Second	Third	Total	First	Second	Third	Total
MEXICAN AMERICAN								
Weeks	47.6	47.8	47.4	47.6	42.4	43.6	44.7	43.5
Hours per week	41.5	42.0	41.7	41.6	37.3	37.7	36.9	37.3
NON-HISPANIC WHITE								
Weeks	48.8	48.8	49.1	49.0	46.4	46.4	46.2	46.2
Hours per week	44.9	43.9	44.2	44.2	37.7	36.8	37.4	37.4
BLACK								
Weeks	48.2	47.0	46.9	46.9	46.8	42.1	45.5	45.5
Hours per week	41.8	41.3	41.3	41.4	39.4	36.7	37.8	37.9
OTHER HISPANIC								
Weeks	48.7	48.7	48.7	48.6	45.7	46.7	47.3	45.8
Hours per week	42.5	41.8	42.0	42.2	37.6	39.2	37.8	37.8
ASIAN								
Weeks	49.2	47.0	48.0	48.7	45.9	43.2	46.0	45.6
Hours per week	42.5	39.2	43.1	42.2	39.0	37.9	39.1	38.9

Source: Author's weighted tabulations from the March 1999 Current Population Survey.
Notes: Includes persons age sixteen to sixty-four who are not attending school, living in group quarters, or serving in the armed forces.

Table 16 Percentage of Full-Time, Year-Round Workers in 1998, by Generation

	MALE				FEMALE			
	First	Second	Third	Total	First	Second	Third	Total
Mexican American	73.4%	67.4%	71.3%	71.9%	51.8%	49.9%	57.4%	53.6%
Non-Hispanic white	76.4%	75.7%	76.2%	76.2%	61.5%	54.7%	56.6%	56.7%
Black	77.4%	63.2%	70.5%	71.0%	70.2%	48.0%	61.7%	62.0%
Other Hispanic	77.7%	66.3%	74.0%	75.5%	60.6%	59.2%	59.8%	60.3%
Asian	78.3%	56.5%	70.0%	75.0%	60.5%	38.3%	62.5%	58.1%

Source: Author's weighted tabulations from the March 1999 Current Population Survey.
Notes: Includes persons age sixteen to sixty-four who worked in 1998 and were not attending school or living in group quarters. Full-time, year-round work is at least fifty weeks and more than thirty-five hours per week.

Table 17 Reasons for Working Part Time in 1998, by Generation

	MALE				FEMALE			
	First	*Second*	*Third*	*Total*	*First*	*Second*	*Third*	*Total*
Could find only part-time work	11.9%	3.8%	5.9%	9.8%	7.9%	11.9%	7.4%	8.6%
Wanted part-time work	2.0%	8.6%	9.2%	4.2%	5.5%	18.0%	26.8%	14.2%
Slack work	58.2%	62.1%	55.0%	57.9%	63.1%	52.3%	37.1%	53.4%
Other reason	27.9%	25.6%	29.9%	28.1%	23.6%	17.7%	28.7%	23.9%

Source: Author's weighted tabulations from the March 1999 Current Population Survey.
Note: Includes Mexican Americans age sixteen to sixty-four who worked part time and were not attending school or living in group quarters.

males than Mexican immigrants, but relative to other third-generation workers, Mexican American males have the third highest percentage of full-time work. Thus, among all ethnic groups, immigrant males are more commonly full-time, year-round workers than are either second- or third-generation workers.

Mexican American women, on the other hand, are generally the least likely of all women to work full-time year-round. Fewer than 54 percent work most of the year, whereas 57 to 62 percent of women of other ethnicities do so. Unlike Mexican American men, third-generation women are the most likely generation to be full-time, year-round workers.

The fact that many Mexican Americans did not work full time may be due either to an inability to find full-time work or to a preference for part-time work. Table 17 tabulates the reasons why Mexican Americans held part-time jobs in 1998. The major reason was **slack work** conditions, that is a reduction in work hours due to slow business. More than 50 percent of all part-time workers found themselves with part-time work because of this situation, and the second most common reason for part-time work was some unspecified reason. With the exception of the first generation, more part-time workers desired part-time work than were forced to accept it for lack of full-time employment. Nevertheless, the majority of those who work part time do so for reasons outside of their control.

Preference for part-time work grows with each generation. Among male immigrants, for example, the preference for part-time work is the lowest (2 percent) of all Mexican Americans (about 9 percent). The difference is most striking among women, however. Only about 6 percent of the first generation desired part-time work, but 18 and 27 percent of the second and third generations, respectively, sought such work. These outcomes may result in lower wages among third-generation workers.

▌ Occupational Patterns

The type of job an individual holds determines not only the wages he or she earns, but also long-term job stability and prospects for economic mobility. At the same time, however, a person's job type is an outcome of the interplay of **human capital** variables, job search and job matching, social networks, and in certain cases, timing. Human capital variables include education and training, language ability, and other traits that enhance a worker's productivity. The search for a new job entails not only actively job hunting, but also using various technologies effectively to find the appropriate job. The search may be conducted by visiting employment agencies, phoning prospective employers, or "hitting the streets." The job search is successful if the employer and employee are matched in terms of qualifications and job requirements. Only when the job is agreeable to both parties is a job offered and accepted. Many workers learn about jobs through informal means, such as when a current worker either passes along information about job vacancies to friends or relatives, or recommends friends and relatives to fill a position. The importance of some of these variables is discussed in greater detail later in the chapter.

Table 18 presents the distribution of each generation of workers in all ethnic groups across seven broadly defined occupation types. Generally speaking, Mexican American males are concentrated in the **blue-collar,** labor-intensive occupations and are less visible in the **white-collar,** professional occupations. For example, 28 percent of second-generation Mexican Americans are operators, fabricators, or laborers, whereas only 13 percent work in professional or managerial occupations. On the other hand, the opposite is true of non-Hispanic whites and Asians—they are heavily concentrated in professional occupations.

Whereas table 18 contains a wealth of information for interethnic comparisons, figures 14 and 15 condense this information for Mexican American men and women, respectively. There are more Mexican American men in operator, fabricator, and laborer occupations (such as drilling and boring-machine operators) than in any other type of occupation, with about 30 percent of each generation of men employed in this sector. More than 20 percent of all Mexican American men work in precision produc-

Table 18 Distribution of Occupation Type, by Generation and Gender in 1998

	MALE				FEMALE			
	First	Second	Third	Total	First	Second	Third	Total
PROFESSIONAL, MANAGERIAL, AND SPECIALIZED OCCUPATIONS								
Mexican American	4.1%	13.4%	14.3%	8.2%	6.2%	17.4%	22.5%	14.7%
Non-Hispanic white	42.7%	41.8%	31.0%	32.0%	36.1%	40.0%	35.6%	35.9%
Black	21.6%	20.1%	15.2%	15.9%	27.5%	45.5%	23.4%	24.0%
Other Hispanic	14.2%	32.5%	24.0%	18.0%	14.9%	33.5%	30.3%	19.9%
Asian	39.1%	30.8%	39.3%	38.5%	36.0%	45.3%	47.4%	38.1%
TECHNICAL, SALES, AND ADMINISTRATIVE SUPPORT								
Mexican American	6.4%	19.2%	17.3%	11.2%	19.5%	48.4%	42.0%	33.9%
Non-Hispanic white	16.8%	20.0%	19.7%	19.6%	31.9%	41.7%	40.9%	40.6%
Black	14.7%	34.0%	18.3%	18.2%	25.3%	32.4%	36.9%	36.2%
Other Hispanic	16.9%	34.0%	24.9%	20.2%	32.2%	47.5%	41.1%	35.7%
Asian	22.8%	30.2%	20.4%	23.2%	30.2%	43.2%	35.7%	31.9%
SERVICE								
Mexican American	16.3%	12.2%	12.5%	14.7%	34.5%	20.5%	24.9%	28.0%
Non-Hispanic white	9.5%	6.9%	7.2%	7.3%	20.1%	11.4%	14.1%	14.2%
Black	20.1%	13.7%	16.0%	16.4%	39.5%	16.0%	27.0%	27.6%
Other Hispanic	16.9%	11.5%	12.9%	15.6%	35.6%	11.6%	19.4%	29.8%
Asian	9.3%	16.3%	8.3%	9.8%	16.1%	9.9%	10.8%	15.0%
FARMING, FORESTRY, AND FISHING								
Mexican American	17.4%	6.2%	5.6%	12.6%	9.4%	2.7%	1.0%	4.8%
Non-Hispanic white	1.4%	2.1%	3.2%	3.1%	1.1%	0.5%	1.0%	1.0%
Black	2.7%	0.0%	2.7%	2.6%	0.8%	0.0%	0.2%	0.2%
Other Hispanic	4.0%	0.0%	1.4%	3.1%	0.6%	0.2%	0.2%	0.5%
Asian	1.0%	4.0%	2.9%	1.5%	0.4%	0.0%	1.7%	0.5%
PRECISION PRODUCTION, CRAFT, AND REPAIR								
Mexican American	23.5%	20.8%	22.0%	22.7%	4.3%	1.5%	1.9%	2.8%
Non-Hispanic white	16.1%	17.8%	21.1%	20.7%	2.4%	1.7%	2.1%	2.1%
Black	15.3%	9.7%	14.9%	14.9%	0.6%	2.1%	2.4%	2.3%
Other Hispanic	19.4%	7.7%	18.8%	17.9%	3.1%	1.6%	2.4%	2.8%
Asian	11.3%	7.3%	20.3%	12.0%	3.6%	0.0%	2.0%	3.1%
OPERATOR, FABRICATOR, AND LABORER								
Mexican American	32.3%	28.2%	28.3%	30.6%	26.1%	9.5%	7.7%	15.7%
Non-Hispanic white	13.5%	11.4%	17.9%	17.4%	8.4%	4.7%	6.2%	6.2%
Black	25.6%	22.5%	32.9%	32.1%	6.4%	4.0%	10.1%	9.8%
Other Hispanic	28.7%	14.3%	18.0%	25.2%	13.6%	5.5%	6.5%	11.4%
Asian	16.4%	11.5%	8.8%	15.1%	13.7%	1.7%	2.4%	11.3%

Source: Author's weighted tabulations from the March 1999 Current Population Survey.

Notes: Includes persons age sixteen to sixty-four who are not attending school and who worked in 1998. Occupation is for the job held longest in 1998. Excludes those who were unemployed or previously in the armed forces.

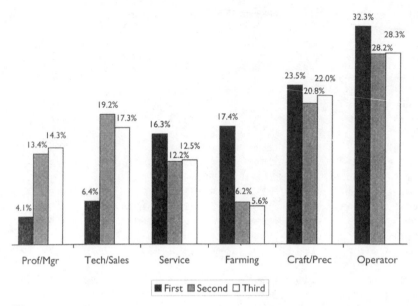

Figure 14. Occupational distribution of Mexican American males by generation. Plotted from data in table 18. (Source: Author's weighted tabulations from the March 1999 Current Population Survey)

tion, craft, and repair occupations (such as cabinet making), making this the second most common type of occupation.

Mexican American men are least likely to work in farming, fishing, and forestry occupations. Although 17.4 percent of immigrants perform this type of labor, less than 7 percent of second- and third-generation Mexican American men do. The low percentage of Mexican American men (and women) in agriculture-related fields contradicts the stereotype of the Mexican worker as a fruit and vegetable picker.

Technical, sales, and administrative support occupations also represent another significant source of employment for Mexican American men, particularly in the second and third generations (19.2 and 17.3 percent, respectively); note that the level for immigrants is much lower, at 6.4 percent. Similarly, professional and managerial occupations account for 13 to 14 percent of second- and third-generation Mexican American male workers, but only 4.1 percent of Mexican immigrants. Lastly, significant percentages of Mexican American men also work in service occupations, with a range from 12 to 16 percent across all generations.

Figure 14 shows that there is a movement away from labor-intensive jobs and into white-collar and technical jobs from the first to the second and third generations. For example, the percentage of workers in operator,

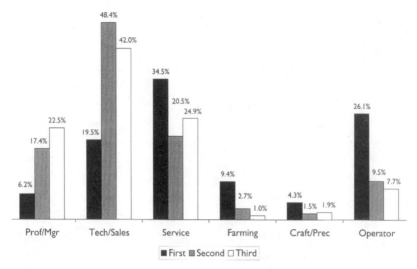

■ Figure 15. Occupational distribution of Mexican American females by generation. Plotted from data in table 18. (Source: Author's weighted tabulations from the March 1999 Current Population Survey)

fabricator, and laborer occupations decreases from 32 to 28 percent between the first and third generations. Similarly, the percentage of workers in professional occupations rises from 4 to 14 percent from the first to third generations. Most of the movement into more prestigious occupations occurs between the first and second generations, although there continues to be an increase into the third generation. These movements are probably associated with the educational levels of each generation.

Figure 15 illustrates that Mexican American women are not as evenly distributed across occupations as men are. More than 40 percent of second- and third-generation Mexican American women work in technically oriented occupations. Another prominent occupation type for these generations is professional and managerial occupations: between 17 and 23 percent work in these types of jobs. Mexican American women are also likely to be employed in service-related occupations (ranging from 21 to 35 percent). Mexican immigrant women are especially likely to be employed in service occupations. Mexican American immigrant women also differ from later generations in that a significant percentage (26 percent) are employed in operator occupations, compared to less than 10 percent for the second and third generations.

Figure 15 also illustrates a shift in occupational composition across generations of women. The movement out of blue-collar and into white-

Topic Highlight: **Opportunities in Real Estate**

Humberto López is a developer who survived the real-estate crash of the late 1980s. López is back on top as one of the most prominent dealmakers and real-estate holders in Tucson, Arizona. He owns and manages four hotels totaling 800 rooms, owns and manages about 2,600 apartment units in twelve complexes, and is managing partner of 1,000 apartments in Phoenix, Yuma, and Dallas. Among his other holdings are two California land-development deals (a 420-home development in San Marcos and a 240-home development in Carlsbad), 40 percent ownership of TransAmerica, a mail-order company in Cleveland with $65 million in sales last year, and a 50 percent interest in the Dorado Country Club in Tucson.

Born in Nogales, Arizona, in 1946, López was raised across the border in Ciudad Obregón, Sonora, until he was twelve, when his father died without a will. The family went from middle class to poor because most of its wealth was lost to lawyers and the Mexican government during probate. His mother moved the family of six back to her native Nogales, Arizona, where López began working, selling newspapers and doing yard work. Throughout high school, he worked forty hours a week at a grocery store, bagging and making deliveries. "We did pretty well in Mexico," he recalled. "But when we came back to the States, our lifestyle changed."

Despite being advised by his high-school counselor to pursue a vocational course, he went to Cochise College with friends. "My counselor didn't think I was capable of going to college and recommended vocational school," López explained. "Several of us who had him as counselor and didn't want to go to vocational school ended up at Cochise, which was new at the time." At Cochise, he took some business courses. He seemed to learn accounting most easily, so he stuck with it and transferred to the University of Arizona. Immediately after graduation, he left Tucson and took an accounting job at Deloitte, Haskins, and Sells in Los Angeles. "When I graduated from the [University of Arizona], I didn't interview in Tucson or Phoenix," he recalled. "I wanted the biggest business with the most exposure. That's because I wanted to find the business for me."

As a certified public accountant, he began requesting real-estate accounts and eventually started getting into the field himself. His first deal involved borrowing $1,000 from an uncle to buy a $3,000 lot. He later sold it for $7,000. Thus began his career in real estate.

Throughout his career, López has found time for civic activities. He has helped not-for-profit organizations raise money and is chairman of the board of advisers for the University Heart Center in Tucson. He was also named Man of the Year by City of Hope and Father of the Year by the Juvenile Diabetes Foundation in Tucson. "I like to give back because the community has been good to me," he said. "I like to give not just money, but my time." (From Higuera 1998). ■

collar occupations is more pronounced among Mexican American women than among men. For example, less than 3 percent of second- and third-generation Mexican American women work in agriculture-related occupations, as opposed to nearly 10 percent of immigrant women, and the percentage of professionals and managers increases from 6 to 23 percent between the first and third generations.

■ Annual Income

The desirability of a job is often highly correlated with its wages. A person's income is generally dependent on education, training, work experience, and other worker attributes that enhance productivity. Although the information in table 19 does not adjust for differences in these human capital characteristics, the mean annual wage information is nonetheless useful.

With a few exceptions, Mexican Americans' annual income is the lowest of all ethnic groups, ranging from roughly $19,400 to $30,000 for men and $13,000 to $18,600 for women. The annual income of Mexican American men ranges from about 50 to 140 percent lower than the income of non-Hispanic white men, and the income of Mexican American women is 35 to 125 percent lower than that of white women.

Table 19 shows improvement in annual income for second- and third-generation Mexican Americans. The second generation earns an average

Table 19 Average Annual Salaries in 1998, by Generation

	MALE				FEMALE			
	First	Second	Third	Total	First	Second	Third	Total
Mexican American	$19,366	$29,965	$28,071	$23,276	$12,910	$18,299	$18,585	$16,194
Non-Hispanic white	$46,297	$51,306	$41,799	$42,441	$29,074	$27,961	$25,121	$25,389
Black	$27,178	$29,935	$27,081	$27,131	$20,927	$25,285	$21,127	$21,173
Other Hispanic	$27,564	$37,658	$32,672	$29,660	$17,849	$25,714	$25,299	$20,125
Asian	$41,410	$31,589	$41,318	$40,502	$25,917	$26,809	$31,098	$26,655

Source: Author's tabulations from the March 1999 Current Population Survey.
Notes: Includes persons age sixteen to sixty-four who are not attending school and who worked in 1998. Excludes persons who were self-employed, worked without pay, or lived in group quarters. Wages and salaries are top-coded by the CPS.

of 35 percent more, and the third earns 31 percent more, than the first generation. The decline in income from the second to the third generation is unexpected. Comparing 1998 income to 1997 income (found in the March 1998 cps) reveals an interesting outcome. Whereas the incomes of first- and third-generation Mexican Americans were comparable between 1997 and 1998, for unknown reasons the income of second-generation Mexican Americans grew substantially; the mean income of the second generation was $24,871 in 1997 but $29,965 in 1998, an increase of 20 percent.

◼ Wages, Human Capital, and Discrimination

Why do Mexican Americans have lower incomes than other groups, especially non-Hispanic whites and Asians? Several possible explanations include discrimination, structural changes in the labor market, such as the loss of high-paying manufacturing jobs overseas, less familiarity with U.S. labor markets among immigrants, lower education levels, less work experience, and other productive characteristics.

Table 20 shows several demographic differences between Mexican-origin and non-Mexican-origin populations in education, work experience, union membership, and English ability. Comparing Mexican Americans to non-Hispanic whites, it is clear that Mexican Americans average less education and less experience, and are less likely to belong to a union or speak English very well. For example, third-generation Mexican American men

Table 20 Selected Worker Characteristics, by Generation and Gender

	MALE				FEMALE			
	First	Second	Third	Total	First	Second	Third	Total
MEXICAN AMERICAN								
Schooling (years)	9.1	12.1	12.1	10.4	9.2	12.3	12.4	11.1
Work experience (years)	19.3	16.1	17.5	18.4	20.9	15.8	17.9	18.7
Union membership	1.1%	1.7%	2.7%	1.7%	0.5%	2.1%	1.4%	1.2%
Speaks English very well	18.4%	85.7%	90.6%	57.7%	—	—	—	—
NON-HISPANIC WHITE								
Schooling (years)	14.1	14.3	13.6	13.6	13.8	13.9	13.6	13.6
Work experience (years)	20.3	21.4	20.0	20.1	22.4	22.0	20.2	20.4
Union membership	2.4%	4.2%	4.1%	4.0%	2.7%	3.4%	2.8%	2.8%
Speaks English very well	75.7%	99.5%	99.9%	99.2%	—	—	—	—
BLACK								
Schooling (years)	12.6	13.7	12.7	12.7	12.8	14.2	13.0	13.0
Work experience (years)	19.8	14.7	19.0	19.0	19.4	13.0	18.9	18.8
Union membership	6.8%	0.0%	4.7%	4.9%	4.6%	6.3%	2.9%	3.1%
Speaks English very well	—	—	99.8%	—	—	—	—	—
OTHER HISPANIC								
Schooling (years)	11.4	13.6	12.7	11.9	11.9	14.1	13.0	12.3
Work experience (years)	20.6	11.2	17.3	18.9	21.3	11.2	18.9	19.6
Union membership	1.3%	2.5%	2.8%	1.7%	1.4%	1.9%	1.4%	1.5%
ASIAN								
Schooling (years)	14.3	14.0	14.3	14.3	13.9	14.7	14.4	14.1
Work experience (years)	18.4	9.4	19.1	17.7	19.8	10.8	18.1	18.8
Union membership	2.7%	2.4%	3.2%	2.7%	2.5%	0.0%	6.3%	2.8%

Sources: English proficiency data are from Trejo (1997), based on the November 1989 Current Population Survey; all other data are author's weighted tabulations from the March 1999 CPS.

Notes: Includes persons age sixteen to sixty-four who are not attending school and who worked in 1998. Excludes persons who were self-employed or worked without pay. Sample weights are used.

average 12 years of education, 18 years of work experience, 3 percent union membership, and 91 percent speak English very well. In contrast, third-generation non-Hispanic whites average 14 years of schooling, 20 years of work experience, 4.1 percent union membership, and 100 percent speak English very well. Therefore, it is not unreasonable to expect that these differences would account, at least to some extent, for the lower relative incomes of Mexican Americans.

Table 21 examines the effect of various demographic characteristics on the hourly wages of Mexican Americans and non–Mexican Americans. The Average Log Hourly Wage section gives the mean of the logarithm of

Table 21 Average and Adjusted Hourly Wages, by Generation

	MALE			FEMALE		
	First	*Second*	*Third*	*First*	*Second*	*Third*
AVERAGE LOG HOURLY WAGE						
Mexican American	2.09	2.39	2.39	1.90	2.18	2.20
Non–Mexican American	2.59	2.82	2.67	2.33	2.54	2.39
ADJUSTED LOG HOURLY WAGE[1]						
Mexican American	2.58	2.68	2.64	2.43	2.43	2.42
Non–Mexican American	2.64	2.82	2.76	2.38	2.54	2.49
IMPLIED PERCENTAGE HOURLY WAGE DEFICIT[2]						
Average hourly wage	−39.7%	−34.8%	−24.5%	−14.1%	−29.4%	−18.0%
Adjusted hourly wage	−5.7%	−13.2%	−11.9%	5.4%	−11.1%	−7.0%

Source: Author's weighted estimates from the March 1999 Current Population Survey.

Notes: Sample includes persons age sixteen to sixty-four who are not enrolled in school and who worked in 1998. Excludes persons who were self-employed, worked without pay, or lived in group quarters.

[1]Estimates are from regressions for males and females of log hourly wages on state of residence, central-city/MSA residence, marital status, work experience (quartic), union membership in March 1999, education, Mexican American identifier for each generation, non–Mexican American identifier for each generation, and a constant. Second-generation non–Mexican Americans are the reference group. Hourly wage is defined as total wage and salary earnings divided by the product of number of weeks worked and usual hours worked per week. Wages and salaries are top-coded by the CPS.

[2]If x is the log wage difference between Mexican Americans and non–Mexican Americans, then the implied wage differential is $e^x - 1$.

hourly wage, the common economic measure of wages, and the Adjusted Log Hourly Wage section gives the log of hourly wage adjusted for demographic differences between non-Mexican-origin second-generation workers and all other workers. The bottom rows give the wage deficit of Mexican Americans after demographic differences between them and second-generation non-Mexican-origin workers are eliminated. Given that the average log hourly wage of non–Mexican American second-generation workers is 2.82, and second-generation Mexican Americans have a corresponding log hourly wage of 2.39, the implied difference in hourly wages (shown in the bottom panel) is −34.8 percent ($e^{2.39-2.82} = -0.348$). In other words, second-generation Mexican Americans earn an average of 34.8 percent less than non-Hispanic whites. Similarly, first- and third-generation Mexican Americans earn 39.7 percent and 24.5 percent less than non-Mexican-origin workers of the same generation. The results show that certain demographic factors—given in the notes of the table—explain between 87 and 94 percent of the lower wages of Mexican Americans.

One reason why adjusted wages decline for Mexican Americans between the second and third generations is a difference in years of experience. As shown in table 20, second-generation Mexican Americans have less work experience than their third-generation counterparts. To calculate the adjusted wages, both generations are given the same years of experience as second-generation non–Mexican Americans (approximately 21.4 years). Doing so increases the experience of second-generation workers more than third-generation workers, resulting in a −0.04 log point lower in adjusted wages for the second generation (2.68 compared to 2.64).

In terms of relative adjusted wages, first- and third-generation Mexican Americans make the biggest gains: first-generation men and women earn 5 to 6 percent less than comparable non-Hispanic workers, whereas third-generation workers earn about 7 to 12 percent less. These figures are considerably less than the average wage deficits.

Unfortunately, the fact is that real-world observed wages (i.e., "average" wages) stagnate from the second to the third generation for both Mexican Americans and non-Hispanic whites. However, contrary to the experience of whites, whose income is significantly lower in the third generation, the wages of Mexican Americans do not decline, and in the case of women, they actually increase. Undoubtedly, the reduction in wages is partly due to a higher percentage of part-time workers in the third generation. For this reason, the adjusted wage deficit of Mexican Americans shows improvement from the second to the third generation.

■ Discussion

Two possible explanations exist for the wage differential between Mexican Americans and European Americans: systematic discrimination against Mexican Americans in the labor market or differences in workers' productive characteristics. Several other studies have reached the same conclusion presented here; namely, that worker characteristics explain about 95 percent of the wage differential between European Americans and Mexican Americans (Cain 1986; Ehrenberg and Smith 1994; Reimers 1985; Trejo 1997). One particularly significant characteristic distinguishing Mexican American from European American men is high English proficiency.

Trejo (1997) suggests that factoring in English language proficiency further reduces the wage differential by about 5 percentage points to almost nothing. (English proficiency was not considered in the present analysis due to data limitations.) Trejo also suggests that any remaining wage difference is explained by the ethnic composition of whites—whites of British descent, for example, earn the same as Mexican Americans with the same characteristics, but both groups earn less than whites of Russian descent. He concludes that third-generation Mexican Americans earn lower wages because of lower productive characteristics, especially education and English proficiency, and that there is no evidence of systematic discrimination in wages. In contrast, he does find evidence of wage discrimination against blacks.

This evidence suggests that improving the educational levels of Mexican Americans is one of the most effective ways to reduce the wage gap between them and non-Mexican-origin workers. Improved English language proficiency will also reduce wage differentials, but this variable is highly correlated with education levels. At the same time, the maintenance of Spanish may result in highly sought-after bilingual workers; these workers may experience labor market rewards that are generally not available to monolingual English speakers.

Furthermore, improved education levels are likely to change the industrial and occupational distribution of Mexican Americans—a high-school graduate would not be expected to be an architect or engineer. The labor market can be divided into two markets, primary and secondary, with the primary market being distinguished by better wages, prestige, and stability (Cain 1986; Schiller 1989). Not surprisingly, entrance into the primary labor market is highly correlated with education. Increases in education, English ability, and work experience will more than likely result in more Mexican Americans moving out of the secondary and into the primary labor market.

Even though wage discrimination is not a significant issue for the majority of Mexican Americans, there is evidence of other types of discrimination. Delgado Bernal (1998) and Monroy (1999) provide evidence of pre-labor market discrimination in terms of Mexican American children receiving a lower-quality education. Unfortunately, no definitive study has been undertaken that measures educational discrimination in a statistically meaningful way. For example, is the lower quality of education provided to Mexican American children due simply to the fact that they are poorer, on average, than **middle-class** Americans? After all, poor whites also suffer from low educational levels. Poor populations live in neighborhoods that cannot fund school districts to the same extent as wealthier neighborhoods. The solution to this inequality is unclear. Attempts to equalize spending across school districts actually have had the perverse result of reducing per-pupil spending, which may end up hurting rather than helping poor students (Silva and Sonstelie 1995).

At the hiring stage, Kenney and Wissoker (1994) found that Hispanics and European Americans with nearly identical qualifications applying for entry-level jobs had different outcomes. In particular, European American applicants were more likely to be asked to file a job application, to obtain a job interview, and to be offered the job than Hispanics were. Kenney and Wissoker's study covered only two cities and was not a representative sample of employers, however, so we should be cautious in assuming that the results provide evidence of systematic job discrimination. Nevertheless, these findings indicate that it is imperative to continue enforcement of anti-discrimination laws at all levels.

■ Summary

The labor market situation of Mexican Americans is in some ways encouraging: they are hard working and dedicated to work. On the other hand, they suffer from higher than average levels of unemployment and spend more time looking for work than most other workers. For those who are working, their occupational profile tells a mixed story. The first generation is likely to be concentrated in labor-intensive manufacturing work, but a fair percentage of the second and third generations moves out of these jobs and into white-collar occupations. Still, fewer Mexican Americans work in prestigious jobs than is true for other ethnic groups.

Mexican Americans earn more than 25 percent less than non-Mexican-origin workers, although the wage deficit decreases across generations. The adjusted averages for Mexican Americans improve into the third generation relative to non-Hispanic whites. Much of the gap can be accounted for by differences in education, English language ability, and other worker characteristics. This suggests that a prescription for attaining economic equality is to eliminate educational inequalities. Although the employment and income statistics are bleak, the education information presented in chapter 4 provides some encouraging signs that educational levels are increasing among Mexican Americans. I hope that these educational gains will continue and result in even greater economic gains for the next generation of Mexican Americans. Current Mexican American workers will also see their wages rise as they become older, acquire more work experience, maintain the same levels of labor force attachment, and continue their quest for *buenos días*.

■ Discussion Questions

1. What is the definition of labor force participation? What are two important LFP characteristics of Mexican Americans that distinguish them from other ethnic groups?

2. How do Mexican American male and female workers differ?

3. What types of occupations are Mexican American men most likely to be employed in? What about Mexican American women? How do these occupational patterns relate to the educational issues discussed in chapter 4?

4. What are the unadjusted and adjusted wage deficits of Mexican Americans relative to other workers? Explain how the two are different and what factors lead to these differences.

5. Describe in your own words how education and age are factors in determining wages.

6. What types of discrimination were discussed in this chapter? How might these forms of discrimination affect the wages of Mexican Americans?

■ Suggested Readings

DeFreitas, Gregory. 1991. *Inequality at Work: Hispanics in the U.S. Labor Force*. New York: Oxford University Press.

Delgado Bernal, Dolores. 1998. Chicana/o Education from the Civil Rights Era to the Present. In *The Elusive Quest for Equality: 150 Years of Chicana/Chicano Education*, edited by José F. Moreno. Cambridge, Mass.: Harvard Educational Review Publishing Group.

Monroy, Douglas. 1999. *Rebirth: Mexican Los Angeles from the Great Migration and the Great Depression*. Berkeley: University of California Press.

Segura, Denise A. 1992. Walking on Eggshells: Chicanas in the Labor Force. In

Hispanics in the Workforce, edited by Stephan Knouse, Paul Rosenfeld, and Amy L. Culbertson. Newbury Park, Calif.: Sage.

Silva, Fabio, and Jon Sonstelie. 1995. Did Serrano Cause a Decline in School Spending? *National Tax Journal* 48, 199–215.

Trejo, Stephen J. 1997. Why Do Mexican Americans Earn Low Wages? *Journal of Political Economy* 105, 1235–68.

7

Buenos Días?

THE BOTTOM LINE

I hope the preceding chapters have given you a greater understanding of particular economic issues relevant to the Mexican American community. The majority of the information in the tables and figures has never been presented in this systematic way before. The body of information forms a portrait of the Mexican American population, allowing us to answer such questions as, What are the salient characteristics of Mexican Americans? How different are Mexican immigrants from U.S.–born Mexican Americans? What distinguishes Mexican Americans from other Americans? For the average Mexican American, what are the prospects of becoming part of the **middle class**?

Throughout I have argued that generation status is the primary explanation for the current **socioeconomic status** of Mexican Americans. More than two-thirds of all Mexican Americans are either immigrants or the children of at least one immigrant parent. Because the majority of Mexican immigrants tend to have less education than other immigrants or Americans, Mexican Americans tend to have higher rates of poverty, higher **unemployment rates,** lower annual incomes, and lower overall **wealth.** In addition, the legacy of discrimination against past generations of Mexican Americans has stunted economic development of the Mexican American community. Only recent reductions in discrimination and segregation, together with a greater appreciation of the Mexican American community, have made it possible for all Mexican Americans to begin realizing their aspirations.

The present-day Southwest belonged to Mexico until 1848, except for southern Arizona, which was purchased in 1853. The cultural roots of the Southwest, therefore, have Spanish and Mexican influences. In chapter 2 I argued that Mexican immigration has been a part of the economic and social life of the Southwest and the United States since long before the current migration stream. The factors motivating Mexicans to venture to **el norte** are many. An early factor was the Mexican Revolution from 1910 to about 1920, and from 1942 to 1964 the **Bracero** Program created an immigration tradition that transcended both political boundaries and legal barriers. The low wages in Mexico coupled with the existence of these **international migration networks** has promoted immigration.

Once immigrants reach the United States, immigrant **enclaves** are particularly important sources of employment and cultural and familial support. Over time, however, the trend is for immigrants to move out of primary enclaves and into less segregated areas. Similarly, the labor market situation of immigrants changes with length of residence in the United States. **Wage assimilation** is observed for immigrants regardless of their year of arrival, but pre-1980 immigrants have wage profiles that more closely resemble the wages of non-immigrants. This conclusion might surprise those who believe that Mexican immigrants are doomed to be poor and, by implication, dependent on government support. In fact, chapter 3 shows that the fiscal impact of immigrants is at worst minimal and more than likely is positive. Another stereotype is that **undocumented immigrants** are different from legal Mexican immigrants. In fact, undocumented immigrants are not that different—many are women, children, and older persons who enter the United States illegally because of barriers to legal immigration. Illegal immigration is fueled by U.S. government restrictions on immigration and an unwillingness to accept that a unique relationship exists between the United States and Mexico. Only through mass legalizations, such as those during the 1950s and 1980s, has the U.S. government tried to address undocumented immigration in a realistic manner. The rise in anti-immigrant sentiments over the past twenty years or so is prompting many of these legalized immigrants as well as long-established immigrants to become U.S. citizens. The political impact of this new block of voters has already been felt in many local and national elections, and the major political parties are now actively recruiting Mexican American voters.

As discussed in chapter 4, evidence of improvement across generations is observed in education. Providing strong evidence that Mexican Americans were denied access to education in the past, younger and third-generation Mexican Americans not only have more education than other Mexican Americans, but they also have education levels that approach those of whites. Unfortunately, there is no clear-cut prescription for eliminating the existing education gap between non-Hispanic whites and Mexican Americans. However, the common denominators are found in successful students and schools with tough academic standards and high educational expectations, parental involvement, motivated students, and caring teachers and administrators.

Chapter 5 dealt with issues of income and poverty. There is much evidence to refute the notion that Mexican Americans are trapped in a cycle of poverty. Measures of income and poverty show much improvement from the first to third generations. Still, Mexican Americans have some of the lowest incomes of all ethnic groups, and their poverty rates are among the highest of all ethnic groups. Despite this fact, Mexican Americans are disproportionately less likely to participate in government assistance programs.

Another gauge of the relative position of Mexican Americans, given in chapter 5, is the accumulation of wealth and assets, as measured by home-ownership and **dividend** income. Although every generation of Mexican Americans has less wealth than other Americans of their generation, each succeeding generation accumulates more wealth than the preceding one. Continued improvement hinges not only on Mexican American participation in financial markets, but also on earnest outreach and education programs by financial institutions. With regard to housing markets, the government must continue to ensure that lending institutions do not discriminate, while lending institutions must continue to adapt to the unique financing strategies used by Mexican American families, such as families pooling their resources to buy a house.

Finally, chapter 6 presented various labor market issues, including labor force participation, occupational status, income, and explanations for the lower wages of Mexican Americans. Of note are the findings that Mexican Americans have one of the highest labor force participation rates of any group, demonstrating the strong work ethic of the Mexican American people. Unfortunately these rates also reflect higher than average unemployment rates among Mexican Americans. One positive interpretation, however, is that Mexican Americans are closely linked to work, so those who are unemployed do not disengage from the labor market or become discouraged and leave the labor force. Instead, they persist in looking for work, even though it takes them longer to find a job. The factors that lead to their higher unemployment rate—inexperience due to the youthfulness of the population and lower levels of education—also explain about 90 percent of their lower wages. Other studies find that English ability accounts for an additional 5 percentage points of the difference, and that third-generation Mexican Americans earn wages comparable to those of European Americans. Such evidence suggests that economic mobility can be accomplished through higher levels of **human capital.**

In conclusion, the quest for economic prosperity is a two-way street: Mexican Americans must strive for prosperity, but the opportunities need to exist. In the past, Mexican Americans were systematically denied economic opportunities and had to fight for even small improvements (Vélez-Ibáñez 1996). Since the Civil Rights Movement of the 1960s, however, Mexican Americans have found that the road is becoming more and more a two-way street. Although the economic status of Mexican Americans still falls short of that of the rest of the nation, many indicators point to an upward progression from one generation to the next. The quest for *buenos días* may yet succeed.

■ Discussion Questions

1. Why is generational status important for the economic assimilation of Mexican Americans? How are third-generation Mexican Americans not the same as third-generation non–Mexican Americans?

2. In your opinion, what are the most important ways that generational status affects the economic assimilation of Mexican Americans?

3. Do you believe that Mexican Americans will differ from other ethnic groups in the ways that they assimilate or acculturate, both socially and economically?

4. What are you doing to reach *buenos días*?

◼ GLOSSARY

acculturation: Process by which members of one culture develop and absorb the traits of another culture, creating a new culture with traits of both cultures. Usually, members of the minority culture absorb more characteristics of the dominant culture than vice versa, although the dominant culture also absorbs some traits from the minority culture.

amnesty: Legal permanent residence granted under IRCA for immigrants who had resided in the United States since January 1, 1982, and to Special Agricultural Workers, who had lower residency requirements (*see also* Immigration Reform and Control Act).

assets: Goods or rights to goods with monetary value that a person owns, such as a home, car, or stocks.

assimilation: The process by which a minority group becomes like the majority group. Generally, assimilation implies the loss of the minority group's characteristics. In economics, assimilation refers to the attainment of parity in economic measures, such as wages or education.

blue-collar job: Generally, a manufacturing or other job requiring manual labor, such as a laborer or construction worker.

bracero: Mexican who participated in the Bracero Program (1942–1964), which granted specified numbers of work permits to Mexicans in order to eliminate labor shortages, primarily in agriculture.

Chicana/Chicano: A person of Mexican descent living in the United States. The term emphasizes pride in the Mexican American culture, history, and indigenous roots, as well as an interest in activism.

cholo: A member of a Mexican American subculture that is rebellious in nature and does not identify with traditional Mexican, American, or Chicano values.

coyote: Smuggler of undocumented immigrants.

cultural deficit model: A now-refuted theory that Mexican American culture fails to provide the tradition and expectations for success in education and society.

displacement effect: Theory postulating that immigrants force natives out of jobs or reduce the wages of natives. Thus, for every immigrant who gets a job, a native loses his or her job.

dividend: A share of a company's profits paid to a stockholder.

education ratio: The ratio of education between two groups, in this case Mexican Americans and non-Hispanic whites. Ratios close to 1.0 reflect convergence in educational achievement.

educational assimilation: The convergence of educational attainment relative to non-Hispanic whites.

el norte: Literally, "the north," a reference to the United States.

employer sanctions: Penalties levied by the U.S. federal government against employers who knowingly hire undocumented workers.

enclave: Area or neighborhood with a majority population of persons of the same culture, language, or nationality.

entry without inspection (EWI):   Describes a person who entered the United States without a visa, usually across the border at a point other than through a port of entry.

family-preference provision: Immigration legislation granting direct relatives of U.S. citizens and legal residents preferential treatment over other prospective immigrants, including an expedited immigration process. Between 1965 and 1990, 80 percent of all visas were allocated for relatives of U.S. citizens and legal residents, but this percentage was lowered in 1990. Two other groups receiving preferential status under immigration law are those with specific job skills and refugees.

full-time work: A job that requires thirty-five or more hours of work per week.

Gadsden Purchase: An agreement signed in 1853 by which the United States purchased from Mexico parts of southern Arizona and New Mexico for $10 million to facilitate the construction of a railroad line.

gross national product (GNP):   The total market value of goods and services produced by a nation during a specified time period; per capita GNP divides this total across the population to obtain an average per person.

human capital: Productive skills and abilities of workers that are valued by employers, such as training, education, and experience.

human capital model: Theoretical and applied model which states that earnings depend on the levels of investment individuals make in skills such as education.

immigrant optimism: A positive attitude about the opportunities available to persons in the United States who have a strong work ethic and an education.

Immigration Reform and Control Act (IRCA):   A federal law passed in 1986 that granted widespread amnesty to undocumented Mexican immigrants already in the United States while imposing penalties on U.S. employers who knowingly hire illegal immigrants and increasing border enforcement.

international migration networks: Informal and formal networks that facilitate the exchange of social support and information regarding immigration, employment, and housing between immigrants in the United States and communities in Mexico.

labor force participation (LFP):   A measure of the individuals in the labor force, including persons with a (full-time or part-time) paying job and those actively searching for work.

Mexican American: A person of Mexican descent born or living in the United States.

middle class: Describes households that have a per capita income of at least $16,203 or that own their home.

naturalization: The process by which an eligible immigrant (broadly, a person with at least five years of permanent residence) becomes a naturalized citizen of the United States.

overstayers: Immigrants who remain illegally in the United States after their visas (student, tourist, work, etc.) have expired.

part-time work: A job that generally requires less than thirty-five hours of work per week.

pollero: A smuggler of illegal immigrants; typically refers to the driver of a smuggling vehicle.

Porfirio Díaz: Mexican dictator (1876–1911) who implemented economic policies that negatively affected the living standard of peasant farmers. His tenure and policies are collectively termed El Porfiriato.

poverty status: Officially, when an individual or family's income is below an amount specified by the federal government as the poverty line, which is adjusted for family size among other factors.

pull factors: Economic, social, political, and other conditions in a receiving country that drive people to immigrate there.

push factors: Economic, social, political, and other conditions that drive people to leave their country of origin.

slack work: Work that is less than the usual amount due to slow business conditions.

socioeconomic status: A measure of a person's economic position and social condition, based on the parent or parents' education, family income, family size, and other important indicators.

Treaty of Guadalupe Hidalgo: The treaty that ended the war between the United States and Mexico (1846–48). It annexed to the United States half of Mexico, now the current U.S. Southwest, for $15 million.

underclass: A term used to describe a population that becomes trapped in a cycle of poverty due to characteristics such as long-term unemployment, lack of training and skills, and a negative outlook regarding mobility.

undocumented immigrant: An immigrant who is in the United States illegally, either through overstaying his or her visa or entering the country without inspection.

unemployment rate: The number of persons without work who are actively looking for a job as a percentage of the total number of labor force participants.

wage assimilation: A process through which immigrants come to earn the same wages as comparable U.S.–born workers.

wealth: The value of all a person's assets (goods with monetary value).

white-collar job: Generally, an office or professional occupation that does not require manual labor, such as a teacher or office clerk (*see also* blue-collar job).

■ REFERENCES

Abraído-Lanza, Ana, Bruce P. Dorhenwend, Daisy S. Ng-Mak, and Blake J. Turner. 1999. The Latino Mortality Paradox: A Test of the "Salmon Bias" and Healthy Migrant Hypotheses. *American Journal of Public Health* 89, 1543–48.

Annerino, John. 1999. *Dead in Their Tracks: Crossing America's Desert Borderlands.* New York: Four Walls Eight Windows.

Bartel, Ann P. 1989. Where Do the New U.S. Immigrants Live? *Journal of Labor Economics* 7, 371–91.

Borjas, George J. 1982. The Labor Supply of Male Hispanic Immigrants in the United States. *International Migration Review* 17, 343–53.

——. 1991. *Friends or Strangers: The Impact of Immigrants on the U.S. Economy.* New York: Basic Books.

——. 1994. The Economics of Immigration. *Journal of Economic Literature* 32, 1667–1717.

——. 1995. Ethnicity, Neighborhoods, and Human-Capital Externalities. *American Economic Review* 85, 365–90.

——. 1996. The Earnings of Mexican Immigrants in the United States. *Journal of Development Economics* 51, 69–98.

Borjas, George J., and Marta Tienda. 1985. Introduction. In *Hispanics in the U.S. Economy,* edited by George J. Borjas and Marta Tienda. Orlando, Fla.: Academic Press.

Borjas, George J., and Stephen J. Trejo. 1991. Immigrant Participation in the Welfare System. *Industrial and Labor Relations Review* 44, 195–211.

Cain, Glen G. 1986. The Economic Analysis of Labor Market Discrimination: A Survey. In *Handbook of Labor Economics,* edited by Orley Ashenfelter and Richard Layard. Vol. 2. New York: Elsevier Science Publishers.

Carter, Thomas P., and Roberto D. Segura. 1979. *Mexican Americans in School: A Decade of Change.* New York: College Entrance Examination Board.

Catão, Luis A. V. 1998. Mexico and Export-Led Growth: The Porfirian Period Revisited. *Cambridge Journal of Economics* 22, 59–78.

Chapa, Jorge. 1988. The Question of Mexican American Assimilation: Socioeconomic Parity or Underclass Formation? *Public Affairs Comment* 35, 1–14.

——. 1989–90. The Myth of Hispanic Progress: Trends in the Educational and Economic Attainment of Mexican Americans. *Journal of Hispanic Policy* 4, 3–18.

Chapa, Jorge, and Richard R. Valencia. 1993. Latino Population Growth, Demographic Characteristics, and Educational Stagnation: An Examination of Recent Trends. *Hispanic Journal of Behavioral Sciences* 15, 165–87.

Chávez, Linda 1991. *Out of the Barrio: Toward a New Politics of Hispanic Assimilation.* New York: Basic Books.

Chiswick, Barry R. 1978. The Effect of Americanization on the Earnings of Foreign-Born Men. *Journal of Political Economy* 86, 97–921.

Danini, Carmina. 1998. Mexican Law on Dual Citizenship Kicks In. *San Antonio Express-News,* March 19.

DeFreitas, Gregory. 1985. Ethnic Differentials in Unemployment among Hispanic Americans. In *Hispanics in the U.S. Economy,* edited by George J. Borjas and Marta Tienda. Orlando, Fla.: Academic Press.

———. 1991. *Inequality at Work: Hispanics in the U.S. Labor Force.* New York: Oxford University Press.

Delgado Bernal, Dolores. 1998. Chicana/o Education from the Civil Rights Era to the Present. In *The Elusive Quest for Equality: 150 Years of Chicana/Chicano Education,* edited by José F. Moreno. Cambridge, Mass.: Harvard Educational Review Publishing Group.

DeSipio, Louis, and Rodolfo O. de la Garza. 1998. *Making Americans, Remaking America: Immigration and Immigration Policy.* Boulder, Colo.: Westview Press.

Domínguez, Robert. 1999. Financial Futures. *Hispanic,* January–February, 38–44.

Ehrenberg, Ronald G., and Robert S. Smith. 1994. *Modern Labor Economics: Theory and Public Policy.* 5th ed. New York: HarperCollins College Publishers.

Fligstein, Neil, and Roberto M. Fernández. 1985. Educational Transitions of Whites and Mexican Americans. In *Hispanics in the U.S. Economy,* edited by George J. Borjas and Marta Tienda. Orlando, Fla.: Academic Press.

Freeman, Gary P., and Frank D. Bean. 1997. *At the Crossroads: Mexican Migration and U.S. Policy,* edited by Frank D. Bean, Rodolfo O. de la Garza, Bryan R. Roberts, and Sidney Weintraub. New York: Rowman & Littlefield.

Funkhouser, Edward. 1995. The Geographic Concentration of Immigrants and Assimilation. Department of Economics, University of California, Santa Barbara. Working paper.

———. 1996. The Fiscal Impact of Immigration on the States: What Have We Learned? Paper presented at the Eighty-Eighth Annual Conference on Taxation Held under the Auspices of the National Tax Association–Tax Institute of America, San Diego, Calif., October 8–10, 1995, 53–58.

Funkhouser, Edward, and Stephen J. Trejo. 1995. The Labor Market Skills of Recent Male Immigrants: Evidence from the Current Population Survey. *Industrial and Labor Relations Review* 48, 792–811.

Gandara, Patricia. 1995. *Over the Ivy Wall: The Educational Mobility of Low-Income Chicanos.* Albany: State University of New York Press.

García, Ignacio M. 1997. *Chicanismo: The Forging of a Militant Ethos among Mexican Americans.* Tucson: University of Arizona Press.

García y Griego, Manuel. 1996. The Importation of Mexican Contract Laborers to the United States, 1942–1964. In *Between Two Worlds,* edited by David G. Gutiérrez. Wilmington, Del.: Jaguar Books.

González, Arturo. 1998. Mexican Enclaves and the Price of Culture. *Journal of Urban Economics* 43, 273–91.

——. 2000. The Education of Immigrant Children: The Impact of Age at Arrival. Mexican American Studies and Research Center, the University of Arizona. Working paper.

González, Arturo, and Adela de la Torre. 2000. The Education and Labor Market Outcomes of Minorities in Arizona: Implications for National and State Policy Makers. Mexican American Studies and Research Center, the University of Arizona. Working paper.

González, Juan L. Jr. 1985. *Mexican and Mexican American Farm Workers: The California Agricultural Industry.* New York: Praeger.

González-Baker, Susan. 1996. Mexican Immigration in the 1980s and Beyond: Implications for Chicanos. In *Chicanas/Chicanos at the Crossroads: Social, Economic, and Political Change,* edited by David Maciel and Isidro D. Ortiz. Tucson: University of Arizona Press.

Gutkind, Efraim. 1986. *Patterns of Economic Behaviour among the American Poor.* London: Macmillan.

Hamann, Volker. 1999. International Labour Migration and Regional Development in Mexico. Paper presented at the Fourth International Congress of the Americas, Puebla, Mexico, October 1999.

Hanson, Gordon H., and Antonio Spilimbergo. 1999. Illegal Immigration, Border Enforcement, and Relative Wages: Evidence from Apprehensions at the U.S.–Mexico Border. *American Economic Review* 89, 1337–57.

Hartman, Pamela. 1999. Law Ships Vietnam Vet back to Mexico. *Tucson Citizen,* April 24, p. 1A.

Hayes-Bautista, David. 1993. Mexicans in Southern California: Societal Enrichment or Wasted Opportunity? In *The California-Mexico Connection,* edited by Abraham F. Lowenthal and Katrina Burgess. Stanford, Calif.: Stanford University Press.

——. 1996. Poverty and the Underclass: Some Latino Crosscurrents. In *Reducing Poverty in America: Views and Approaches,* edited by Michael R. Darby. Thousand Oaks, Calif: Sage.

Hernández, Norma G. 1973. Variables Affecting Achievement of Middle School Mexican-American Students. *Review of Educational Research* 43, 1–39.

Hevesi, Dennis. 1999. "Immigrants' Dream Is Finding a Home Inside the Golden Door." *New York Times News Service,* January 24. http://www.latinolink.com/news/99/0124nhom.htm (November 12, 1999).

Higuera, Jonathan J. 1998. Developer Stands Tall after Crash: Local Mogul 'Toughed' It Out, Hitting the Top of the Market. *Tucson Citizen,* May 18, p. 1A.

Hopkins, Connie. 1999. The Whitewashing of Higher Education. *Hispanic,* June, 34–40.

Kao, Grace, and Marta Tienda. 1995. Optimism and Achievement: The Educational Performance of Immigrant Youth. *Social Science Quarterly* 76, 1–19.

Kenney, Genevieve M., and Douglas A. Wissoker. 1994. An Analysis of the Correlates of Discrimination Facing Young Hispanic Job-Seekers. *American Economic Review* 84, 674–83.

Laguna, Jesse. 1994. Latinos Want a Tighter Border, Too. *Los Angeles Times,* September 23, Op-Ed section.

LaLonde, Robert J., and Robert H. Topel. 1992. The Assimilation of Immigrants in the U.S. Labor Market. In *Immigration and the Work Force: Economic Consequences for the United States and Source Areas,* edited by George J. Borjas and Richard B. Freeman. Chicago: University of Chicago Press.

Lee, Don. 1998. Housing Crunch: Asians, Latinos Create a New Market Model. *Los Angeles Times,* August 30, Business section, p. 1.

Massey, Douglas S. 1986. The Settlement Process among Mexican Migrants to the United States. *American Sociological Review* 51, 670–84.

———. 1987. Do Undocumented Migrants Earn Lower Wages than Legal Immigrants? New Evidence from Mexico. *International Migration Review* 21, 236–73.

———. 1999. International Migration at the Dawn of the Twenty-First Century: The Role of the State. *Population and Development Review* 25, 303–22.

Meier, Matt S., and Feliciano Ribera. 1993. *Mexican Americans/American Mexicans.* New York: Hill and Wang.

Meissner, Doris. 2000. "Testimony of Commissioner Doris Meissner, Immigration and Naturalization Service (INS), before the Committee on Appropriations Subcommittee on Commerce, Justice, State, and the Judiciary, United States Senate Concerning the President's Fiscal Year 2001 Budget Request." http://www.ins .usdoj.gov/graphics/aboutins/congress/testimonies/2000/meissner2k0307.pdf (September 28, 2000).

Mincy, Ronald B. 1994. The Underclass: Concept, Controversy, and Evidence. In *Confronting Poverty: Prescriptions for Change,* edited by Sheldon H. Danzinger, Gary D. Sandefur, and Daniel H. Weinberg. Cambridge, Mass.: Harvard University Press.

Monroy, Douglas. 1999. *Rebirth: Mexican Los Angeles from the Great Migration and the Great Depression.* Berkeley: University of California Press.

Monto, Alexander. 1994. *The Roots of Mexican Labor Migration.* Westport, Conn.: Praeger.

Moore, Joan. 1989. Is There a Hispanic Underclass? *Social Science Quarterly* 70, 265–85.

Mora, Marie T. 1997. Attendance, Schooling Quality, and the Demand for Education of Mexican Americans, African Americans, and Non-Hispanic Whites. *Economics of Education Review* 16, 407–18.

O'Neill, Stephanie. 1994. Casa, Sweet Casa: Latino Home Buyers Are the Fastest-

Growing Group in the Los Angeles County Real Estate Market. *Los Angeles Times,* December 4, Real Estate section, p. 1.

Ovando, Carlos J., and Virginia P. Collier. 1998. *Bilingual Education and ESL Classrooms: Teaching in Multicultural Contexts.* Boston, Mass: McGraw-Hill.

Paulin, Geoffrey D. 1998. A Growing Market: Expenditures by Hispanic Consumers. *Monthly Labor Review* 121, 3–21.

Reimers, Cordelia W. 1985. A Comparative Analysis of the Wages of Hispanics, Blacks, and Non-Hispanic Whites. In *Hispanics in the U.S. Economy,* edited by George J. Borjas and Marta Tienda. Orlando, Fla.: Academic Press.

——. 1992. Hispanic Earnings and Employment in the 1980s. In *Hispanics in the Workforce,* edited by Stephen Knouse, Paul Rosenfeld, and Amy Culbertson. Newbury Park, Calif.: Sage.

——. 1997. The Progress of Mexican and White Non-Hispanic Immigrants in California and Texas, 1980 to 1990. *The Quarterly Review of Economics and Finance* 37, 315–43.

Reiner, Cathy. 1994. An Immigrant's Dream—Buying a Home in the United States Is a Critical Turning Point, but the Process Can Be Difficult for Those from Other Cultures. *Seattle Times,* December 11, p. E1.

Rivera-Batiz, Francisco L. 1999. Undocumented Workers in the Labor Market: An Analysis of the Earnings of Legal and Illegal Mexican Immigrants in the United States. *Journal of Population Economics* 12, 91–116.

Rochin, Refugio I., and Adela de la Torre. 1996. Chicana/os in the Economy: Issues and Challenges Since 1970. In *Chicanas/Chicanos at the Crossroads: Social, Economic, and Political Change,* edited by David R. Maciel and Isidro D. Ortiz. Tucson: University of Arizona Press.

Rodríguez, Gregory. 1996. *The Emerging Middle Class.* Institute for Public Policy, Pepperdine University.

Romo, Harriet, and Toni Falbo. 1996. *Latino High School Graduation: Defying the Odds.* Austin: University of Texas Press.

Rothenberg, Daniel. 1998. *With These Hands.* New York: Harcourt Brace.

Rumberger, Russell. 1991. Chicano Dropouts: A Review of Research and Policy Issues. In *Chicano School Failure and Success: Research and Policy Agendas for the 1990s,* edited by Richard R. Valencia. New York: The Falmer Press.

Sánchez, George J. 1993. *Becoming Mexican American.* New York: Oxford University Press.

Santos, Richard, and Patricia Seitz. 1992. School-to-Work Experience of Hispanic Youth. *Contemporary Policy Issues* 10, 65–73.

Schiller, Bradley. 1989. *The Economics of Poverty and Discrimination.* 5th ed. Englewood Cliffs, N.J.: Prentice Hall.

Schmader, Toni, Brenda Major, and Richard H. Gramzow. 1998. Coping with Ethnic Stereotypes in the Academic Domain: Perceived Injustice and Psychological

Disengagement. Department of Psychology, the University of Arizona. Working paper.

Secretaría de Educación Pública. 1998. *Informe de labores.* México, D.F.: SEP.

Segura, Denise A. 1992. Walking on Eggshells: Chicanas in the Labor Force. In *Hispanics in the Workforce,* edited by Stephan Knouse, Paul Rosenfeld, and Amy L. Culbertson. Newbury Park, Calif.: Sage.

Silva, Fabio, and Jon Sonstelie. 1995. Did Serrano Cause a Decline in School Spending? *National Tax Journal* 48, 199–215.

Smith, James P., and Barry Edmonston, eds. 1997. *The New Americans: Economic, Demographic, and Fiscal Effects of Immigration.* Washington, D.C.: National Academy Press.

Solis, Julie. 1995. The Status of Latino Children and Youth. In *Understanding Latino Families: Scholarship, Policy, and Practice,* edited by Ruth E. Zambrana. Thousand Oaks, Calif.: Sage.

Solórzano, Daniel G., and Ronald W. Solórzano. 1995. The Chicano Educational Experience: A Framework for Effective Schools in Chicano Communities. *Educational Policy* 9, 293–314.

Soltero, José M. 1996. *Inequality in the Workplace: Underemployment among Mexicans, African Americans, and Whites.* New York: Garland Publishing.

Suárez-Orozco, Marcelo M., and Carola E. Suárez-Orozco. 1995. The Cultural Patterning of Achievement Motivation: A Comparison of Mexican, Mexican Immigrant, Mexican American, and non-Latino White American Students. In *California's Immigrant Children: Theory, Research, and Implications for Educational Policy,* edited by Ruben G. Rumbaut and Wayne A. Cornelius. San Diego, Calif.: University of California San Diego.

Tienda, Marta, and Zia Liang. 1994. Poverty and Immigration in Policy Perspective. In *Confronting Poverty: Prescriptions for Change,* edited by Sheldon H. Danzinger, Gary D. Sandefur, and Daniel H. Weinberg. Cambridge, Mass.: Harvard University Press.

Tobar, Hector. 1998. Special Report: As Political Participation Begins to Catch up with a Wave of Immigration and Naturalization in Southeast L.A. County . . . Communities See a Surge in Latino Voter Registration. *Los Angeles Times,* April 26, Metro section, p. 1.

Trejo, Stephen J. 1997. Why Do Mexican Americans Earn Low Wages? *Journal of Political Economy* 105, 1235–68.

U.S. Bureau of the Census. 1999. "Poverty Thresholds in 1998." http://www.census.gov/hhes/poverty/threshld/thresh98.html (October 31, 1999).

U.S. Immigration and Naturalization Service. 1997. *Statistical Yearbook of the Immigration and Naturalization Service, 1996.* Washington, D.C.: Government Printing Office.

——. 1999a. *Annual Report: Legal Immigration, Fiscal Year 1998.* Washington, D.C.: Government Printing Office.

——. 1999b. "Illegal Alien Resident Population." http://www.ins.usdoj.gov/graph ics/aboutins/statistics/illegalalien/index.htm (October 31, 1999).

Vargas, Zaragosa. 1993. *Proletarians of the North: A History of Mexican Industrial Workers in Detroit and the Midwest, 1917–1933.* Berkeley: University of California Press.

Vélez-Ibáñez, Carlos G. 1993. U.S. Mexicans in the Borderlands: Being Poor without the Underclass. In *In the Barrios: Latinos and the Underclass Debate,* edited by Joan Moore and Raquel Pinderhughes. New York: Russell Sage Foundation.

——. 1996. *Border Visions: Mexican Culture of the Southwest United States.* Tucson: University of Arizona Press.

Vernez, Georges, Allan Abrahamse, and Denise Quigley. 1996. *How Immigrants Fare in U.S. Education.* Santa Monica, Calif.: Rand Corporation.

The World Bank. 1997. *World Development Indicators.* Washington, D.C.: The World Bank.

Zsembik, Barbara A., and Daniel Llanes. 1996. Generational Differences in Educational Attainment among Mexican Americans. *Social Science Quarterly* 77, 363–74.

■ Index

123–24; generational attainment of, 63–65, 95; higher, 68–71, 116; and income, 71–73, 122–23; language and, 75–76; levels of, 61–63; and migration, 16, 34–36; public spending and, 50–51; secondary, 65–68; and socioeconomic status, 73–74, 76–77, 78; and wages, 33–34, 122, 127–28

education ratio, 63–64, 68

employers: and IRCA, 27–28

employer sanctions, 27–28, 54

employment, 20, 53; and education, 71–73

enclaves, 44, 45–46, 127

English-language use, 76; wage differential and, 121–22

entry without inspection (EWIS), 51, 52

ethnic groups, 122; immigration of, 19, 20; poverty rates of, 128

Europeans: as immigrants, 20, 31

EWIS. *See* entry without inspection

exploitation: of undocumented workers, 15–16

export sector: growth of, 18–19

families, 10, 53; educational attainment and, 69, 77; immigration and, 23–24, 25, 26, 29; income of, 81–84; poverty rate and, 85, 87, 91; public assistance and, 88–89

family-preference provisions, 25, 32

Federal National Mortgage Association (Fannie Mae), 99

first generation, 7, 9. *See also* generational status

Florida, 45, 51

food stamp program, 50, 90

Gadsden Purchase, 13

gender: and labor force participation, 107–8, 109–12; occupation type and, 113 (table), 115, 117

gender distribution, 7; of Mexican immigrants, 39, 40 (table)

generational status, 126, 127; education and, 76, 77, 95; income and, 81–84, 117–18; occupation type and, 113 (table), 114–15; poverty and, 85–86; and public assistance, 88–89; wages and, 118–21; work levels and, 109, 111–12

gold rush: California, 17

González, Héctor, 38

government assistance programs. *See* public assistance

graduate education, 69, 70

Great Depression, 5, 20–21, 31

Great Society, 88

gross national products, 15

health, 9, 39, 40, 92

Hernández, Armida, 99

Herrera, Norberto, 13, 15

high school, 73; graduation from, 65–68

hip-hop groups, 104

Home Mortgage Disclosure Act, 99

homeownership, 97–99, 128

Houston, 45

human capital, 47, 112, 129

Huntington Park, 58

Illegal Immigration Reform and Immigration Responsibility Act (IIRIRA), 29, 31, 32

Illinois, 3, 45

immigrant optimism theory, 76, 81, 95

immigrants: demographics of, 39–41; income and poverty of, 42–44, 85; settlement patterns of, 44–47

immigrant status, 6, 7

immigration, 10–11, 13–14; before 1910, 17, 19–20; economic impacts of, 48–49; phases of, 23–24; undocumented, 15–16, 26–27, 32, 38, 52–53; U.S. policies of, 24–26, 31
Immigration Act (1990), 29
Immigration and Nationality Act, 24, 25
Immigration and Naturalization Service (INS), 26, 29, 31, 51–52
Immigration Reform and Control Act (IRCA), 16, 53; citizenship and, 56, 57; regulations under, 27–28, 32
income, 10, 11, 126; education and, 71–74, 122–23; generational status and, 81–84; of immigrants, 23, 24; jobs and, 117–18; of Mexican immigrants, 42–44; socioeconomic status and, 93, 95
income distribution, 80, 81–84, 86, 92
industrialization, 18
INS. See Immigration and Naturalization Service
international migration networks, 15, 24, 44, 127
IRCA. See Immigration Reform and Control Act

Japanese, 19
jobs. See occupations
Johnson, Lyndon, 88

labor, 4, 9, 23; Bracero Program and, 21–22; and immigration, 19–20, 31
labor force participation (LFP), 9–10, 128; rates of, 105–9
labor market, 104, 127, 128; activity in, 105–9; discrimination in, 121–23; immigrants and, 49–50
labor movement: and Bracero Program, 22–23

Laguna, Jesse, 48, 50
land reform: under Porfiriato, 18, 19
language: education and, 75–76; and wage differential, 121–22
LFP. See labor force participation
loans: home, 98–99
López, Humberto, 116–17
Los Angeles, 5, 14, 45, 46

macroeconomy: and poverty rates, 94–95
Madero, Francisco, 19
malnutrition, 18
Massachusetts, 3
Medicaid, 50
Medina, Gerardo "Lalo," 104
Mendoza, Javier, 98
Mendoza, Mary, 98
Mendoza, Rafael, 98
Mexican Americans, 3; and Bracero Program, 22–23
Mexican Revolution, 18, 19, 24, 26, 31, 127
Mexicans, 3, 38, 52; immigrant characteristics of, 39–41; income of, 42–44; naturalization of, 55–56, 59; settlement patterns of, 44–47; wage assimilation and, 47–48
Mexico, 15, 17; dual citizenship in, 56–57
Michigan, 3
middle class, 10, 93–94; education and, 73, 122; homeownership and, 97, 99; movement toward, 80–81; purchasing power of, 100–101
Midwest, 3, 4, 20
migration, 16; human capital model of, 32–36
Miller, John, 55
mining, 17, 19, 20

standard of living, 53, 84

stereotypes, 4–5

stocks: ownership of, 97, 100

taxation, 49

technical occupations, 114

Texas, 3, 20, 51; immigration to, 17, 52; Mexicans in, 45, 59

third generation, 7, 9. *See also* generational status

transitional phase, 23

Treaty of Guadalupe Hidalgo, 13

underclass, 5, 10, 80; Mexican Americans as, 91–92

underclass model, 77, 91, 92–93

undocumented immigrants, immigration, 15–16, 26–27, 31, 32, 38, 39, 90, 127; classification of, 51–52; discrimination and, 54–55; history of, 52–53

unemployment rate, 9–10, 92, 105, 108–9, 126, 128

United Farm Workers, 23

upper class, 73

urban sector, 45

Urroz, Jorge, 13, 15

wages, 16, 105, 112; assimilation in, 47–48; demographics and, 118–21, 128–29; education and, 51, 71–73, 123–24; and human capital model of migration, 32–35

wealth, 11, 96, 126, 128; and education, 73–74; indicators of, 97–101

welfare programs: generational status and, 88–89; Mexicans and, 44, 50, 90

work: full- and part-time, 105, 107–8, 109–12. *See also* occupations

work ethic, 109

World War II, 21, 31

■ ABOUT THE AUTHOR

Arturo González is an economist at the Mexican American Studies and Research Center at the University of Arizona, where he has taught since 1997. He received his Ph.D. in economics from the University of California, Santa Barbara, and his bachelor's degree in economics from the University of California, Los Angeles. Winner of the Lancaster Award for best dissertation of 1996–1998 in the Social Sciences at the University of California, Santa Barbara, he was also nominated for the National Council of Graduate Schools and University Microfilm International Distinguished Dissertation Award, 1996–1998. González's research focuses on the education and labor market outcomes of immigrants and Latinos in the United States. He has published in the areas of Mexican enclaves, English language acquisition, education, and immigrant earnings. His current research projects examine the role of community colleges in the postsecondary education and labor market experience of Latinos and the English-language acquisition by male and female immigrants.

Mexican Americans and the U.S. Economy is a volume in the series The Mexican American Experience, a cluster of modular texts designed to provide greater flexibility in undergraduate education. Each book deals with a single topic concerning the Mexican American population. Instructors can create a semester-length course from any combination of volumes, or may choose to use one or two volumes to complement other texts.

Additional volumes deal with the following subjects:

Mexican Americans and Health
Adela de la Torre and Antonio Estrada

Chicano Popular Culture
Charles Tatum

Mexican American History
Juan García

Chicanos and the Environment
Devon Peña

Mexican American Identity
Aida Hurtado and Patricia Gurin

For more information, please visit
www.uapress.arizona.edu/textbooks/latino.htm